BIG BEN

The Bell, the Clock
and the Tower

BIG BEN

THE BELL, THE CLOCK AND THE TOWER

PETER MACDONALD

FOREWORD BY
TAM DALYELL MP,
FATHER OF THE HOUSE

SUTTON PUBLISHING

First published in the United Kingdom in 2004 by
Sutton Publishing Limited · Phoenix Mill
Thrupp · Stroud · Gloucestershire · GL5 2BU

British Library Cataloguing in Publication Data
A catalogue record for this book is available from the British
Library.

ISBN 0-7509-3827-7

Typeset in 11.5/15pt Melior.
Typesetting and origination by
Sutton Publishing Limited.
Printed and bound in England by
J.H. Haynes & Co. Ltd, Sparkford.

Contents

CONTENTS

List of Illustrations

Foreword

In my forty-two years as a Member of Parliament, I have looked up to Big Ben thousands of times from New Palace Yard. However, between 1962 and 1976 I fear I took the chimes for granted. That is until Big Ben went silent. Peter Macdonald puts it with characteristic elegance:

> The Great Clock had now been operating for some months with the movement supported rather precariously on the two hydraulic jacks and with no chime; it could not be allowed to continue in this fashion. Of course, although silent it is still a beautiful clock, but with no chime it lacked its crowning glory, rather like a blackbird with no song or a rose without a scent. Somehow it had to be restored.

Proudly standing at the corner of the Palace of Westminster, the world-famous icon Big Ben is familiar to many and perhaps almost too familiar to those, like myself, who have passed it daily and whose days are regulated by its chimes. In his new book, Peter Macdonald has caused me to stop and think about this great monument. He reveals the bitter rivalry, scientific innovation and engineering problems that beset Big Ben during its conception in the 1830s. The struggle for accuracy – unprecedented in such a large outdoor clock, today still one of the largest in the world – remains unsurpassed.

In the most momentous events of the twentieth century Big Ben played its part. I well remember, as a young boy, its victory peal signalling the end of the Second World War. It has also had a vital role in more light-hearted occasions. Who does not remember the celebrations for the Queen's Golden Jubilee? And how strange it would be if the New Year was not rung in by its great bell.

By delving into the history behind Big Ben, Peter Macdonald has shed new light on this famous but perhaps taken-for-granted symbol. I, for one, will not now hear the chimes nor see the impressive tower without a greater sense of the fascinating history and magnificent achievement that is Big Ben.

Tam Dalyell

Tam Dalyell, 2004

Acknowledgements

The help of the following during my research is gratefully acknowledged: British Library Newspaper Library for press reports and programme details from *Radio Times*; Ursula Carlyle, Curator and Archivist of the Mercers' Company for the history of the Royal Exchange; Robert Crayford, Archivist at St Paul's Cathedral for the history of the clock and bells; John Davis, Senior Archive Assistant at the BBC Written Archives Centre for broadcasting schedules; Guildhall Library for the history of E.J. Dent & Company; House of Lords Record Office for the building of the Great Clock and tower and details of the temporary chimes; Alan Hughes and Mandy Davis of the Whitechapel Bell Foundry for the inscription on Big Ben, its statistics and those of the quarter bells and Britain's heaviest bells; Professor Frank King, University Bellringer and Keeper of the University Clock for the history of Great St Mary's Church, the clock and bells; Matthew Read, Assistant Curator of Horology at the Royal Observatory, Greenwich for the history of the Greenwich Time Ball and the telegraph

link to Westminster; Brian Tipper, Horological
Engineer at the Palace of Westminster for details
of regulating and maintaining the Great Clock.

Introduction

Big Ben is a character, a personality, the very heart of London, and the clock tower at the Houses of Parliament has become the symbol of Britain, known and loved around the world. It is the nation's clock, instantly recognisable, brought into British homes every day to give the time signal on BBC Radio 4, its strokes used to introduce ITV's *News at Ten*, and seen and heard frequently on other news and current affairs programmes. It has always been popular with authors and film makers and the famous scene in the screen adaptations of John Buchan's novel *The Thirty-Nine Steps*, together with appearances in many other films and documentaries, has done much to establish the clock as a cultural icon. Nowadays, almost every guidebook to London features a picture of Big Ben on the cover – it represents the capital, along with the black taxi and the Routemaster bus.

But Big Ben is more than a clock – as part of Britain's heritage it has long been established as the nation's timepiece, its chimes heralding almost every broadcast of national importance, announcing both the nation's joy and the nation's grief. Yet despite its Gothic appearance, the clock tower, and indeed the present Houses of Parliament, came into existence only after fire destroyed the ancient Palace of Westminster in the 1830s and plans for the new Houses of Parliament included a fine clock on the northern tower. It was to be a king among clocks, towering over Westminster and striking the first blow of each hour to within a second of the time, an accuracy which most leading members of the clockmaking fraternity believed to be unattainable on such a large turret clock where four sets of very heavy hands are subject to the mercy of all weathers. In an effort to overcome this seeming technical impossibility the Worshipful Company of Clockmakers even appealed to Parliament for less severe specifications. But this request was refused and after much uncertainty and delay the clock was eventually designed, not by a well-known and much respected professional clockmaker, but by the most gifted and resourceful of amateurs whose determination and inventive genius were to be almost entirely responsible for the magnificent clock's completion.

In the mid-nineteenth century, great strides were being made in the fields of science and engineering – among them the pioneering of photography, the discovery of Neptune in 1846 and the development of the railway network throughout the United Kingdom. For the science of horology there could be no greater challenge than the building of the largest and most accurate public timepiece in the world; and it is a lasting tribute to the Victorian engineers and craftsmen not only that such accurate running was achieved but also that it has been maintained from the very first tick in 1859 right up to the present day. As society developed, there was increasing need for such accuracy; and as the clock may be heard from within the Commons, one of its original purposes was the timing of parliamentary debates.

Big Ben is, of course, the great bell on which the hours are struck, but it has also become the name by which the clock is known. In 1924, daily radio broadcasts of the bells were introduced and, with a few interruptions, they have continued ever since. It is through broadcasting that the music of the chimes has become known universally, and it was during the Second World War, when the time was broadcast most frequently at home and overseas, that the chimes developed such a special significance and their music became known as the 'signature tune of the British Empire'. Today, who can imagine the solemn ceremony from the Cenotaph on Remembrance Day or the joyous celebration of New Year's Eve without the sound of the famous chimes? These chimes have been copied on so many public clocks and countless private ones around the world that there can hardly be a country where they are not found. The melody of Westminster has also served as inspiration to a number of composers, finding its way into the music of Eric Coates and Ralph Vaughan Williams among others.

During its long and distinguished career, the clock has been stopped on very few occasions through a fault of the mechanism – little more than a broken spring or a snapped cable. Even during the Blitz when the House of Commons was totally destroyed and the clock tower sustained superficial damage Big Ben kept going and sent out a daily message of hope and defiance around the world. This was truly the 'voice of Britain' and the sound of the bells did much to boost morale. Despite coming so close to destruction, it is wonderful to recall that Big Ben was not stopped once by enemy action during the Second World War. However, the clock has been brought to a standstill a few times by heavy snow impeding the hands; more amusingly, it was slowed by five minutes on one occasion when a murmuration of starlings settled on one of the minute hands; and it ground to a halt on another when a painter's ladder fouled part of the mechanism. During 1934 and 1956 the clock was out of service for several months for major overhauls and broadcasting duties were taken over by Great Tom, the clock of St Paul's Cathedral. In 1976 a serious mechanical failure almost tore the clock apart, leaving the chimes silent for many months, and once again the cathedral clock proved an admirable deputy on the air. So great was the damage to the mechanism that consideration was given to replacing the movement rather than to repair, but fortunately repair was possible and the Great Clock was restored to full working order in time for the Queen's visit to the Palace of Westminster for her Silver Jubilee in 1977.

A visitor to the clock room might expect to hear the continual rumble of machinery or the grinding of cogs, whereas one is greeted by no more than the stately tick produced every two seconds by the constant swing of the pendulum, to be interrupted on each quarter-hour by the operation of the chiming and striking mechanisms. In fact, the great cog wheels and drive shafts revolve so slowly that they appear stationary. Big Ben is a masterpiece of horological engineering and represents the very pinnacle of turret clockbuilding, setting a standard which has never been surpassed.

For many, the sound of the bells is associated with peace and democracy, hope and stability, yet the clock was born out of uncertain beginnings and its construction was plagued by years of bitter argument and hostility, due mainly to poor relations between clockmaker and architect. First, part of the mechanism had to be redesigned as it was found to be too large to fit into the clock room. This was doubly unfortunate as it contributed directly to the great catastrophe that occurred over a century later. Next, the hour bell cracked while it was being struck experimentally in New Palace Yard. It was broken up and recast, but to an individual shape as it had been discovered that the shaft through which it was to be raised to the belfry was too narrow to admit a bell of conventional design. Then, after the clock had been completed it would not go – the hands were found to be too heavy for the mechanism to drive and they had to be replaced with lighter sets. Finally, as if all this had not been enough, after the clock had been started the recast hour bell cracked within just a few weeks of coming into operation and for about two years the hours were struck on the deepest of the quarter bells. Eventually, Big Ben was brought back into use, having been turned so that the crack is away from the hammer. It is this crack which gives the bell its unmistakable tone. The clock was eagerly awaited by Londoners, who were very aware of its progress, just as the modern public followed the building of the Millennium Bridge or the London Eye. The setbacks encountered during the construction of the clock delayed its progress for some years and will no doubt put the reader in mind of similar difficulties experienced with the construction of other projects in recent years. These early troubles overcome, the clock went on to give more than a century of almost trouble-free service.

As Big Ben's 150th anniversary approaches in 2009, the world in which it was conceived has long since disappeared. In the intervening period there have been more technological developments than could ever have been foreseen by even the most progressive and imaginative of nineteenth-century scientists. In horology, clockwork gave way first to electric and then to quartz movements – a modern quartz wristwatch provides the kind of accuracy which would have been inconceivable even just a few decades ago. More recently, radio clocks have become available for domestic use at affordable prices. Some, which are controlled by broadcast impulses, display the time continually and require no correction, even adjusting automatically to Greenwich Mean Time (GMT) and British Summer Time (BST). At the beginning of the twenty-first century, it seems that time is everywhere instantly available. And today's atomic clocks, capable of incomprehensible levels of accuracy, while splitting the second into ever smaller pieces, take timekeeping into an altogether different sphere. In physics, too, so many advances have been made that it has become necessary to redefine the second; it is no longer measured as a fraction (1/86400) of the mean solar day but is reckoned as the duration of many million periods of the radiation of the caesium-133 atom. Despite all this, some things appear never to change. Big Ben has become an integral part of Britain – a national treasure; during almost one and a half centuries as the nation's timekeeper it remains the most celebrated and the most consistently accurate public clock in the world. It is admired by Londoners and visitors alike and the highest standards of maintenance are employed to ensure its survival for future generations.

1

In the Beginning . . .

Had it not been for the fire which destroyed both Houses of Parliament on the night of 16 October 1834, Big Ben might never have been built. Construction was excruciatingly slow and fraught with so much argument, hostility and suspicion that a quarter of a century would elapse between the destruction of the old Palace of Westminster and the completion of the clock.

Before meeting the personalities involved in the designing and building of the Great Clock, in order to set it in context it is worth considering the history of Westminster, the development of horology and, most importantly, the need for accurate timekeeping. Big Ben is not the first great clock to stand by the Thames at Westminster – indeed, the story begins over seven hundred years ago towards the end of the thirteenth century, for it was around this time that a clock was erected in New Palace Yard. Some authorities maintain that this was the first public clock to be built in Britain, but unfortunately no information concerning the mechanism has survived. However, it is likely that the clock was controlled by an early form of verge escapement and that it made use of a foliet, which was a balance bar shaped rather like a dumb-bell. The foliet was the predecessor of the pendulum and it swung horizontally. In fact the pendulum, which swings in the vertical plane and is so familiar nowadays, was not invented until the middle of the seventeenth century. Galileo was believed to have been engaged on the development of a pendulum clock at the time of his death in 1642, but it was the Dutch astronomer and mathematician Christiaan Huygens who completed his design for the first pendulum clock in 1656. His clock is believed to have been made by Samuel Coster during the following year under a patent granted to him by Huygens. Although it is conceded that Huygens was the inventor of the pendulum clock, Galileo's son claimed that the invention was his father's. Contrary to a popular misconception, it is, in fact, the clock that drives the pendulum, whose regular beat enables the clock to maintain time.

The early clock at Westminster is thought to have featured one dial, facing the palace, the hours being indicated by just a single hand as well as being struck upon a bell. The fact that it had a dial is a reflection of the clock's importance. Very early clocks, most of which were used for ecclesiastical purposes, did not possess a dial or hands, relying merely upon the striking of a bell to denote the passing of the hours. In those distant times it was only the nobility and the clergy who could read and write or understand the passage of time as indicated by the movement of a hand upon a dial; the remainder of the population had to rely on the sound of a bell. But the Palace of Westminster was not only the main royal residence, it was also the seat of government, and so the clock had to be designed accordingly. Even so, early turret clocks were very unreliable. They were usually built by blacksmiths and constructed from iron. With no bearings or compensation for changes in temperature, they could vary by perhaps thirty minutes or even more during the course of twenty-four hours and required a daily correction by comparison with a sundial. So, this first clock at Westminster would not have had anything like the accuracy which we would expect today. The bell on which the hours were to be struck was cast around 1290 in the reign of King Edward I and was called Edward of Westminster. It weighed 4 tons, which was a good weight for a bell in the thirteenth century. Although officially called Edward, the bell soon became known as Great Tom. It was to strike the hours at Westminster for almost the next four centuries, during which time it managed to survive a number of minor incidents.

During the early evening of 6 April 1580 an earthquake was felt over a wide area of southeastern England. It was one of the few British earthquakes known to have caused fatalities. In Dover, part of the castle wall was demolished and it is recorded that in London two deaths were caused by falling masonry and that St Paul's Cathedral sustained some damage. At Westminster, Great Tom was set ringing by the force of the tremor, striking itself against the hammer, although the clock appears to have remained unscathed.

However, the clock is thought to have sustained some damage during the Civil War when a small band of Royalists took refuge in the clock tower. It seems that they felt capable of defending the tower in a siege and offered considerable resistance to Cromwell's men, but when their ammunition became exhausted they removed whatever they could from the clock and threw it down in an effort to fend off their besiegers. Eventually, the damage sustained to the mechanism was repaired but the clock was never the same again, or so it is said. It seems that this lack of reliability was to be of great benefit to one man. There is a story that sometime during the seventeenth century, a young soldier named John Hatfield was brought before a court martial, charged with having fallen asleep while on sentry duty one night at Windsor Castle. The soldier maintained that he had not been asleep and in his defence stated that he had heard Great Tom strike thirteen at midnight. Upon enquiry, his statement was found to be correct, the court accepted his evidence and he was acquitted. Windsor is some twenty miles from London and one might wonder how the soldier could claim to have heard the clock at such a distance, but perhaps in former times, at night and before the constant rumble of traffic, it might just have been possible for someone with exceptionally good hearing under the most favourable conditions. That's the story, but it may or may not be true. It certainly seems very unlikely.

Towards the end of the seventeenth century the clock had fallen into such a state of disrepair that it stopped working altogether. In about 1700, the clock tower, which was crumbling to a great extent, was demolished. It is not known what became of the clock or its mechanism, but the bell was sold to St Paul's Cathedral, which had recently been rebuilt by Sir Christopher Wren after the ravages of the Great Fire. Unfortunately, some time elapsed before the bell reached the cathedral, for while being transported along the Strand it fell from its carriage near the road which has subsequently been called Bell Yard, and lay shattered. Two attempts by Phillip Wightman to recast the bell some years later proved unsuccessful, but eventually in 1716 it was recast satisfactorily by Richard Phelps at the Whitechapel Bell Foundry. By the provision of some additional metal, he increased its weight to more than 4½ tons and installed it in the south-west tower of St Paul's, where it remains to this day. For almost three hundred years, Great Tom has sounded the hours as they have been struck from the cathedral, both by the earlier clock and by the present one. But the bell is not the only connection between the clocks at Westminster and St Paul's, as will be shown later.

After Great Tom's departure at the end of the seventeenth century there was to be no great clock at Westminster for more than two hundred and fifty years, during which time horology saw many developments. As already noted, during the middle of the seventeenth century the pendulum had been invented and it was eagerly adopted as the standard by clockmakers. Around the same time, the English physicist Robert Hooke invented the anchor, or recoil escapement. Previously, the verge was the only form of escapement in use and the introduction of the anchor was the first step towards making the pendulum an accurate timekeeper. Most importantly, in 1675, King Charles II had established the Royal Observatory at Greenwich for the purpose of establishing longitude at sea. Estimating the position of a ship when in sight of land was not difficult, but doing the same after many weeks or months at sea and with no landmarks had hitherto proved impossible. Finding the longitude was the most pressing scientific problem of the day for it was known that accurate navigation would bring supremacy at sea. The King's warrant therefore charged John Flamsteed, the first Astronomer Royal, 'to find out the so much desired Longitude of Places for perfecting the art of navigation'.

By the beginning of the eighteenth century so many ships and their cargos were being lost as a result of seafarers being unable to determine their position that the situation was desperate indeed.

In 1714, in an effort to remedy the situation, Parliament offered a prize of £20,000 to any person who could establish a method which would resolve the longitude to within one half of one degree, a distance of some thirty-five miles at the equator, decreasing to about twenty-two miles at the latitude of London. This prize represented a magnificent sum in the eighteenth century – today it would be worth well over £1 million – and many schemes were put forward, some of which were not worthy of even the slightest consideration. One of the most bizarre suggestions involved using a solution known as the 'powder of sympathy'. This powder, if it ever existed, was reputed to possess almost miraculous healing properties, but unfortunately, not without pain. It was claimed not only that dipping a patient's bandage, or even an implement which had caused an injury, into the powder would hasten the healing of a wound but also that it would continue to do so even over great distances. This scatterbrain scheme for finding the longitude required sending on every voyage a dog which had been wounded with a knife. The knife would be left ashore in the custody of some responsible person who would dip it into the powder every day at noon. On feeling the pain, the dog would yelp in sympathy, thus providing the captain with the time at his home port. Needless to say, this scheme, in common with so many others which were proposed, had no scientific foundation and could not be taken seriously.

In fact, it was not until John Harrison set to work to develop his chronometers that any advance was made. Harrison reasoned that if a ship could carry a clock which maintained the time of its home port, the mariner could establish his longitude by comparing the difference between clock time and local noon which occurs when the sun reaches its greatest altitude above the horizon. Time is longitude and longitude is time – the idea was simple but the solution was virtually impossible. Because of the pitching and rolling of a ship, a pendulum clock would be useless at sea, so Harrison spent the greater part of his working life perfecting the chronometer, a precision instrument driven by a spring rather than by a weight. Harrison was a perfectionist who worked alone and was never satisfied. After the decades of frustration and rejection, which he had experienced with the development and presentation of his three earlier models, he completed his H4 chronometer in 1759. It was a masterpiece of engineering which became the forerunner of all marine chronometers. The H4 underwent many exhausting trials, and after several months at sea it had accumulated an error of a mere few seconds and provided the determination of longitude to within limits far more stringent than those which had been laid down by Parliament. Harrison had made the greatest possible contribution to navigation, yet his reward for finding the longitude was given very grudgingly, and by instalments, his final payment being made when he was eighty years of age; even then it was received only after he had appealed to the king, George III. It has been said that Harrison gave Britain the Empire, for without the development of the chronometer it is unlikely that she would have become such a great seafaring nation. Harrison's chronometers H1 to H4 are among the nation's treasures and may be seen at the Old Royal Observatory, Greenwich, where they are on permanent exhibition. His final endeavour, H5, is on display in the Clockmakers' Museum at the Guildhall in London. Harrison was also one of Britain's most gifted clockmakers and produced some splendid examples, his finest turret clock probably being that at Brocklesby Park in Yorkshire.

As society developed so there was an ever greater need for the accurate measurement of time. Almost every village and town had a clock, usually on the church or an important civic building. Even the most modest of these clocks would probably have been accurate to within a few minutes. The clock face would have been the same as we know today, with two hands, one indicating the hours and the other the minutes, and the dial showing the twelve hours. The hands would move in a 'clockwise' direction, that is to say, the direction of the shadow cast by the gnomon on any horizontal sundial, or even by a simple stick in the ground, situated in European latitudes, which is where horology developed.

9

Because time varies with longitude, there were considerable differences in the time shown on clocks in the east of the British Isles and those in the west. These differences had become apparent through the timing of stage coaches, but it was the coming of the railways in the 1830s and 1840s which demonstrated beyond any doubt the need for uniformity. The effect was not so noticeable on lines running to the north, but the greatest problems were experienced by the Great Western Railway on their services to the West Country – for example, the time in Plymouth is more than a quarter of an hour behind that in London. As most lines radiated from the capital, the railway companies preferred to operate their schedules to London time which came to be known in its more diplomatically acceptable form as railway time. In 1848 a bill which sought the introduction of a standard time was brought before Parliament, but it faced such strong opposition, particularly from local and regional interests, that it was thrown out. Local time was always implied unless it was stated otherwise. A court case in the 1850s illustrated just how confusing was this state of affairs when it had to be retried after the defendant arrived late for the hearing, but claiming that he was on time by the clock in his home town! Indeed, it was not until 1880 that the Definition of Time Act was passed and Greenwich Mean Time became the standard for the whole of the British Isles. Even when Big Ben started its long and distinguished career in 1859 it showed London time while clocks in other parts of Britain gave their local time. Today, we are so accustomed to having the time displayed accurately at our fingertips that we do not stop to consider how different things would have been in the early part of the Victorian period when there was no radio, no television, no telephone or satellite communication and consequently no broadcast time signals.

However, the concept of providing a time signal was beginning to be discussed and in 1833 the Astronomer Royal, John Pond, instituted the Greenwich Time Ball as a means of providing a signal to shipping on the River Thames. A marine timekeeper is designed to keep time, but before setting out on a long voyage, it was necessary to know the time in the first place. At Greenwich, ships' chronometers could be compared with the observatory clock. This would have to be done indirectly; as any movement of the chronometer might affect its rate, a pocket watch would be taken ashore and used as a go-between.

During the early part of the nineteenth century, there appears to have been a number of experiments which were undertaken at various locations involving the sending of a time signal from the shore for the benefit of ships anchored at harbour. The modes of operation were very rudimentary and included the waving of a flag or the firing of a gun. In 1829, an experimental time ball which was controlled by a signal from the

11

Royal Naval College in the dockyard was erected at the entrance to Portsmouth harbour. This appears to have been the precursor of a regular time signal because in October 1833 the Admiralty issued the following Notice to Mariners:

> The Lords Commissioners of the Admiralty hereby give notice that a ball will henceforth be dropped every day from the top of a pole on the Eastern Turret of the Royal Observatory at Greenwich, at the moment of one o'clock PM mean solar time. By observing the first instant of its downward movement, all vessels in the adjacent reaches of the river as well as in most of the docks, will thereby have an opportunity of regulating and rating their chronometers. The ball will be hoisted half-way up the pole, at five minutes before one o'clock, as a preparatory signal, and close up at two minutes before one.

As the observatory had been built upon the hill in Greenwich Park, it is easily visible from the Thames, so the ball was set upon a tower on Flamsteed House and operated in the following manner. In accordance with the Notice to Mariners, at five minutes to one the ball was hoisted from its 'dropped' or resting position to half way up the pole by an assistant operating a pulley far below in the observatory, as an indication that the hour was approaching. Then at 12.58 it was hoisted the remainder of the way to the top. Finally, at one the ball was released by another assistant located in front of the clock in the observatory and fell to the 'dropped' position, giving the time.

One might wonder why the ball was not operated at twelve – after all, this is the middle of the day and it would seem to be the most appropriate hour at which to indicate the time. However, it was at noon that the astronomers were occupied in determining the time, so the ball was set to give the signal one hour later, at one. The time ball apparatus was constructed by Maudslay & Field of London, and although the original ball was replaced by the present one in 1919, its appearance has remained virtually unchanged. However, since 1852 the instant of the drop has been controlled by the Galvano-Magnetic Clock built by the master clockmaker Charles Shepherd and installed in the observatory during that year. This clock uses galvano-magnetic circuits to operate the time ball and to send impulses which control various 'slave clocks' in different parts of the observatory. One of these is situated near the main entrance, and is sometimes known as the 'gate clock'. Here a visitor to the observatory can check Greenwich Mean Time. The clock features a twenty-four hour dial and displays GMT throughout the year. In 1960 the raising of the time ball also became automatic. Nor has operation of the ball been without incident; on one occasion in the 1850s it was blown down during a gale. More recently an anemometer has been installed and in very severe conditions the time ball is not operated. The time ball was greatly appreciated by the masters of ships anchored along the Thames as it enabled them to set their chronometers without the inconvenience of leaving their vessels. Of course, the observatory is no longer housed in the buildings at Greenwich and vessels today are equipped with global positioning receivers which display the time and their geographic co-ordinates continuously, but the ball is one of the very earliest regular public time signals and it still falls every day making an interesting spectacle. Allowance is made for summer time, the signal being given at one o'clock GMT or BST, whichever is in operation. This was to be the forerunner of other time signals, because with the evolution of the telegraph system the opportunity was taken to develop the transmission of signals for the benefit of other users, mainly the Post Office and the railways.

In the north of Britain, visitors to Edinburgh are often startled by a blast of gunfire at lunchtime followed by the puzzling sight of locals checking their watches. This is the sound of the One o'Clock Gun, a single shot to give the single hour, and fired from the ramparts of the castle, high above the city. Following the example of Greenwich, in 1852 a time ball was erected on the Nelson Monument for the benefit of ships anchored in the nearby port of Leith, the mechanism being controlled by a clock in the Royal Observatory, then situated on Calton Hill. (Since the early part of the twentieth century the Royal Observatory has been housed on Blackford Hill.) In 1858, a local businessman, John Hewitt was elected to the Chamber of Commerce. Hewitt suggested that the effectiveness of the time ball could be enhanced, particularly during periods of poor visibility, by the addition of an audible signal and proposed the introduction of a gun. The Chamber was enthusiastic about this suggestion and soon approved the scheme and a telegraph line was installed between the observatory and the gun at Half Moon Battery in the castle.

The first day of operation in June 1861 was attended by several dignitaries but unfortunately the ceremony turned out to be something of an embarrassment for the city authorities as the gun failed to fire. It also failed on the following day but the initial problems were soon overcome and the gun has been heard regularly ever since. It is fired daily at one o'clock, except on Sundays, Good Friday and Christmas Day. For obvious reasons it did not operate during the two world wars. However, it is fired on Remembrance Sunday at eleven o'clock and again at two minutes past to mark both the beginning and the end of the silence. In 1971, during a performance of the Edinburgh Military Tattoo an explosion weakened the old battlements around Half Moon Battery and since then the gun has been fired from Mills Mount Battery. The original gun, an 18-pounder muzzle-loading cannon, was fired automatically by an impulse from the observatory clock; but today's gun, a 25-lb howitzer, is discharged manually, a duty that has been proudly carried out by Staff Sergeant Tom McKay – District Gunner 'Tom the Gun' – since 1978. Before the Definition of Time Act came into force in 1880, the gun was fired at one o'clock Edinburgh mean time, about thirteen minutes behind Greenwich, but now of course it is fired at one o'clock GMT or BST. It is interesting to see the time ball descend at the instant when the gun is fired; under ideal conditions the report may be heard for some miles. Recently the castle has mounted the One o'Clock Gun exhibition tracing the history of the gun and this is open daily to visitors.

In the nineteenth century it was the practice of the London watch and clock makers to visit the observatory in order to obtain the time, taking with them a watch for the purpose of comparing their regulator with the clock at Greenwich. Eventually the observatory became responsible for conveying the correct time; towards the end of the Victorian era this duty was carried out by Miss Ruth Belville who was known to have been calling on the London clockmakers even up to the first decade of the twentieth century. She became known as the 'Greenwich Time Lady' and carried a pocket watch made by John Arnold, the eighteenth-century watchmaker. A greeting from a customer might go like this: 'Good morning Miss Belville, how's

Arnold?' and she would reply, 'Arnold's five seconds fast today,' or whatever was the error, whereupon the customer would check his regulator. 'Arnold' too has been preserved and is also on display in the Clockmakers' Museum at the Guildhall.

As had happened just over three years previously at the Palace of Westminster, on 10 January 1838 fire destroyed the Royal Exchange in the City of London. (In fact, this was the second Royal Exchange to be burned down; the original building, which dated from the sixteenth century, was consumed in the Great Fire of 1666.) Bells have long been part of the City's heritage and it was considered appropriate to continue this tradition by erecting a fine clock on the newly rebuilt Exchange, while taking advantage of the many recent developments in horology. A contemporary pamphlet announced that 'The clock is to be the best specimen that can be produced, and is intended to furnish the Merchants and Captains of the most accurate record of time in the City of London. It is to be made by Mr Dent, under the direction of the Astronomer Royal, Professor Airy.' (George Airy had succeeded John Pond as Astronomer Royal in 1835.)

Completed in 1845, Edward Dent's clock was constructed to a very high standard and was considered to be the foremost timekeeper in the capital. More significantly, its design was to be instrumental in the construction of the Great Clock at Westminster. The original clockwork mechanism was replaced by an electric movement during the early part of the twentieth century, and more recently this has given way to a radio- controlled quartz device. The clock may be seen in the heart of London's bustling financial quarter, just opposite the Bank of England, where its bells still record the passage of time. Originally, the clock was provided with sufficient bells to play a number of well-known melodies but regrettably much of the chiming mechanism has been allowed to fall into disrepair and nowadays the bells just sound the hours and the quarters. Mounted above the clock tower is a weather vane in the form of a grasshopper, the device of Sir Thomas Gresham, founder of the Royal Exchange.

Despite Dent's obvious enthusiasm for innovation, many of the established clockmakers were rather set in their ways and not willing to consider new ideas. They tended to view any change with suspicion and were concerned to a very great extent with protecting their own interests. But times were moving forward and technology was advancing due to the endeavours of a few progressive men who were not afraid to press ahead in spite of fierce criticism from their peers. This new clock at the Royal Exchange in the City of London had been built to a very high specification. It represented the very latest in horological engineering and demonstrated what could be achieved by the most resourceful and forward-thinking of clockmakers.

Royal palaces do not usually have a clock tower as their most prominent architectural element, but as such a tower had been a feature of the original Palace of Westminster for several hundred years, the opportunity was taken to continue the tradition and erect the finest of clock towers on the new Houses of Parliament. Horology had come a very long way since that early clock was built at Westminster at the end of the thirteenth century and now at the Royal Exchange the people of London had a clock which they could expect to keep time to within very reasonable limits. But for the wider population, time was still kept by the local public clock which had the disadvantage of requiring frequent regulation by comparison with a sundial. This, then, was the state of public timekeeping during the early part of the nineteenth century. Meeting the challenge of building a great turret clock with four sets of hands, its mechanism subject to the vagaries of temperature and weather and yet capable of keeping perfect time, was to be the horologist's ultimate triumph.

2

A Great Clock for Westminster

Over the centuries many people have probably wished that they could destroy the Houses of Parliament and on a fateful night in 1834 two men succeeded, quite by accident, where all others' attempts had failed.

In a storeroom inside the Palace of Westminster a vast amount of exchequer tallies had accumulated. In earlier times these wooden billets had been the Treasury's form of receipt issued against a loan. Each comprised two unequal portions, the Treasury keeping one part and the lender the other. Repayment was made if the two parts fitted (i.e. tallied), after which the Treasury kept both. They became redundant during the early part of the nineteenth century and had been withdrawn over a period of many years, eventually being returned to the Exchequer which was then situated within the Palace of Westminster, where they awaited disposal. Ultimately it was decided to burn them in the large furnace located beneath the House of Lords. The two stokers appointed to carry out the task filled the furnace to the brim and left the tallies to burn. When the flues became blocked the fire soon spread to the store of tallies and, fanned by a strong wind, the flames quickly engulfed the building – with disastrous results.

It is said that the news spread more quickly than the fire and that Londoners flooded in their thousands to watch as the inferno consumed the greater part of the Palace of Westminster. Fire crews operating from floats along the Thames experienced considerable difficulty in gaining strategic positions from which to direct their equipment, as the river was littered with small craft crowded with spectators anxious to obtain the best view of the spectacle. Among them, quite possibly, was the great artist J.M.W. Turner, preparing sketches for his picture *The Burning of the Houses of Parliament*. It has also been said that on that night Charles Barry, the architect, never one to miss an opportunity, was travelling into London and stopped his coach to look at the blaze, wondering, perhaps, whether his services might be required in the building of a new Palace of Westminster. As things turned out, his involvement would be one long battle spanning the last twenty-five years of his life.

Following the disaster, Parliament was prorogued and in November of the following year a Select Committee of the Commons was formed to consider the rebuilding of the Palace. An invitation was issued to architects to enter into an open competition for the design of the new Houses of Parliament, which was to be either in the

Elizabethan or the Gothic style so as to harmonise not only with the ancient Westminster Hall, which had been spared from the flames, but also with the neighbouring Westminster Abbey. The committee examined more than ninety entries, none of which included a clock tower. After due consideration, they concluded in favour of the design submitted by Charles Barry, who was probably the leading architect of the day. There followed some collaboration between Barry and his very gifted assistant Augustus Welby Pugin which resulted in a number of revisions including the addition of a clock on the northern tower, which was to be surmounted by a spire. The scheme, approved by the committee in April 1836, called for a fine clock tower with four faces, each 30 feet in diameter, an hour bell weighing 14 tons and eight quarter bells.

In September 1843, after a delay of more than seven years, work commenced on the construction of the clock tower, but it was another sixteen long and painful years until the Great Clock was completed and Big Ben struck the now familiar hours over the metropolis. In the following year, 1844, the designs of the proposed elevation were exhibited at the Royal Academy. These provoked a good deal of criticism, not only from some Members of Parliament, but also from sections of the public who were concerned about the additional expense involved in providing a clock tower and who suggested that there was no need for a public clock 'when almost every mechanic carries a watch in his pocket'. Despite this opposition it was generally felt that the clock tower would enhance the dignity of the new Houses of Parliament – and in any case the Office of Works had already stipulated that there should be 'a noble clock, indeed a king of clocks, the biggest the world has ever seen, within sight and sound of the throbbing heart of London'. Charles Barry, eager to see his architectural dreams come to fruition, probably regarded the provision of the clock as a trivial addition to what was to become not only a very beautiful but also the constitutionally most important building in the land. In the absence of any instruction to the contrary, he considered that the choice of clockmaker had been left to him, and he approached Benjamin Louis Vulliamy, Clockmaker to the Queen and Master of the Worshipful Company of Clockmakers to prepare the design of the Great Clock. Not surprisingly, this caused rather a stir in the horological world, as many long-established and well-respected clockmakers considered it unfair that such a prestigious contract should be awarded without competition. One of the profession to feel thus disgruntled was Edward John Dent, he who had been so involved in the development of the chronometer, and whose recently completed public clock at the Royal Exchange was proving to be so reliable. A chronometer is a small precision instrument which can operate to a high degree of accuracy; its principal use was on board the ships of both the royal and the merchant navies. Dent had shown that chronometers could be mass-produced while retaining their high degree of accuracy, the resultant saving in cost allowing them to be carried in a far greater number of ships.

In 1846 Dent wrote to the Astronomer Royal, George Airy, who had supervised the building of his clock at the Royal Exchange, to seek a recommendation to enable him to tender for the construction of the new clock at Westminster. Considering Dent to be one of the most advanced and innovative of clockmakers, Airy was pleased to offer his support and he wrote to Viscount Canning, the Chief Commissioner of Works, with a glowing testimonial. This brought a swift response from Canning stating that the Great Clock should be the very best which British science and skill could supply and requesting that the Astronomer Royal be referee for its design. Airy accepted the invitation enthusiastically and drew up a specification of fifteen conditions relating to the general construction and working of the clock. Most clockmakers believed one of these conditions to be unattainable. This condition related to the accurate running which was to be maintained and it demanded a standard which had never before been contemplated, let alone attempted, on such a large turret clock, namely that 'the striking machinery is to be so arranged that the first blow for each hour shall be accurate to a second of time'. In addition, the specification called for the provision of an electromagnetic connection to enable the clock's timekeeping to be telegraphed twice a day to the Royal Observatory at Greenwich, where a record of its performance would be kept. So, some twelve years after the fire which had so mercilessly destroyed the Palace of Westminster, the idea of a new Great Clock, which would be not only the biggest but also the best in the world, was beginning to take shape.

A limited competition was opened to clockmakers and invitations incorporating the Astronomer Royal's specification were sent to three contenders – E.J. Dent & Company, Louis Vulliamy and John Whitehurst of Derby, all well-established concerns that had produced many clocks of fine quality. Vulliamy protested that it would be quite impossible to construct a clock of such a size which would meet the Astronomer Royal's requirements as far as accuracy was concerned. He frequently pointed out, and quite rightly, that there is a world of difference between making an accurate chronometer with its intricate movement and very small hands, which could be operated under controlled conditions, and building a very large turret clock where the mechanism weighs many tons and four sets of very heavy hands are subject to the mercy of the elements. However, Dent and Whitehurst accepted the Astronomer Royal's specification, and tenders were received from both companies later in 1846: Dent's for £1,500 and Whitehurst's for £3,373. Interestingly, Whitehurst, who noted that most striking clocks have either two or four bells on which to chime the quarters, proposed the introduction of five quarter bells. On the hour they would remain silent, giving no warning of the impending strokes. Had this scheme been adopted, it would have seemed very strange indeed. Vulliamy also sent in his designs, which Barry had asked him to prepare, but quoted no tender price. He declared that he never undertook designs or commissions in competition with others and, further, that the clocks proposed by Dent and Whitehurst would be unable to maintain the standard of accuracy which had been demanded by the Astronomer Royal. In 1847, Airy added an extra condition to the original list of fifteen. This required the installation of an electromagnetic apparatus which would produce a current for regulating other clocks at the Palace. Dent required an extra £100 for this device and Whitehurst an additional £150, taking their totals to £1,600 and £3,523, respectively.

Having made a detailed examination of the three sets of plans, Airy reported back to the Chief Commissioner. He appears not to have made any recommendation regarding the acceptance of either tender, leaving the choice of clockmaker to the Commissioner. He did, however, make the following comment about Vulliamy's design:

It is impossible for me to consider Mr Vulliamy as a person who can be employed to construct the clock. I have very carefully examined Mr

Vulliamy's beautiful plans. In regard to the provision for strength, solidity, power and general largeness of dimensions, they are excellent. In regard to delicacy they fail and they fail so much, that I think myself justified in saying that such a clock would be a village clock of a very superior character but would not have the accuracy of an astronomical clock.

Vulliamy never forgave Airy for his description of his design as 'a village clock' and from then on it was warfare. In fact, Vulliamy's dislike of Airy was so intense, it was second only to his hatred of Dent, whom he regarded as a privileged and favoured competitor. Later that year, the London-based firm of Thwaites & Reed applied to put forward a tender, but the commissioners decided that, in view of the time which had elapsed, admitting further tenders would not be appropriate. However, more than a century later, it was to be Thwaites & Reed who would rebuild the mechanism and return the clock to its former glory after the mechanical failure which caused such utter devastation and which could, so easily, have brought about the end of the clock. (Interestingly, shortly after Thwaites & Reed applied to tender, applications were received from two private individuals, Samuel McClennan of London and James Mangan of Cork, for the opportunity to tender for the Great Clock, but these were not taken seriously.)

If any one man can be said to have played the leading role in bringing the clock into existence, that man must surely be Edmund Beckett Denison, QC. A barrister by profession, he was also a gifted amateur horologist – indeed, a respected authority – who had made an extensive study of clock-making and had also written a great deal on the subject. In 1848, Denison, who had taken a keen interest in the proposed building of a great clock ever since the idea had been put forward, wrote to the Chief Commissioner of Works, by now Lord Morpeth, drawing his attention to the considerable delay in providing it. After consulting with the Astronomer Royal, Lord Morpeth, who was well aware of Denison's horological expertise, invited him to become joint referee for the clock's design. Denison accepted the invitation with alacrity and his appointment as joint referee provided the necessary impetus, since his enthusiasm and determination were to prove essential to bring about the Great Clock's completion.

The two referees could not have been more different. Born in 1801, George Biddell Airy was an outstanding scientist who had distinguished himself with many academic achievements while at Cambridge. He entered Trinity College as a sizar in 1819, had been a Senior Wrangler and first Smith's Prizeman in 1823, Lucasian Professor of Mathematics in 1826 and Plumian Professor of Astronomy and Director of the Observatory in 1829. In 1835, while still in his mid-thirties, he became Astronomer Royal, a post which he was to hold for the next forty-six years. In 1836 he was elected a Fellow of the Royal Society and in 1846 was the recipient of the Royal Astronomical Society's gold medal. He had an excellent knowledge of timekeeping, much of which had been gained through his experience in the trials of chronometers. He was knighted in 1872 in recognition of his lifelong contribution to astronomy.

Edmund Beckett Denison was born in 1816 and, like Airy, had been educated at Cambridge. He, too, had followed a distinguished career, but in the legal profession, becoming a QC and a leader of the Parliamentary Bar, one of the most lucrative branches of the profession. His legal adversaries described him as 'a doughty fighter who never seemed to realise when he was beaten'. He was at his very best when a case seemed hopeless. As a very gifted amateur horologist he had designed some first-class clocks and was considered a leading exponent on the subject. He had contributed the section on clocks in *Encyclopaedia Britannica* and his *Rudimentary Treatise on Clocks, Watches and Bells*, published in 1850, became a standard reference work, reprints being available until quite recently. Airy was courteous, mild mannered and considerate – Denison was rather abrasive and never took into account the feelings of others, but both men were absolutely committed to the completion of the Great Clock. As honorary referees, neither received any financial reward for his services; even for Airy the appointment formed part of his official duties as Astronomer Royal.

Denison wasted no time before immersing himself wholeheartedly in this challenging task of constructing the best clock in the world. He immediately undertook a thorough examination of all three designs, Vulliamy's, Dent's and Whitehurst's. He, too, had no use for Vulliamy's plan and after extensive deliberation he wrote to the Chief Commissioner to inform him that he found the design by Dent to be far superior to the others. Even so, he proposed many suggestions for improvements to Dent's original drawing which virtually amounted to a redesign. Had Denison's revisions not been incorporated into the clock's movement, it is unlikely that the prescribed level of accuracy could have been achieved and it is fitting that the inscription along the bedplate in the clock room records Denison as the designer.

A contract was awarded to Edward Dent in January 1852 and work commenced straightaway on the construction of the mechanism. Meanwhile, the Worshipful Company of Clockmakers continued to maintain that the Astronomer Royal's specification had set impossibly high demands as far as the standard of accuracy was concerned and they had, at Vulliamy's instigation, already addressed a memorial to Parliament seeking less severe conditions, but this was given little consideration. Airy was determined that the clock would be built and refused to lower his standards. In a fit of indignation, Vulliamy was reported as saying: 'Dent will never make that clock.' This turned out to be somewhat prophetic, for in March of the following year, 1853, Edward Dent died. By this time, work on the mechanism was well advanced and since most of the crucial designs had been finalised, in the normal course of events Dent's demise would not have affected the progress of the clock.

The firm of E.J. Dent & Company had been founded in 1840 and ran its affairs from three addresses in London. Under the terms of Edward Dent's will, the business would pass to his two stepsons, provided that they took the surname Dent. Richard Dent (previously Rippon) inherited the premises at Cockspur Street while Frederick Dent (also previously Rippon) inherited both the premises in the Strand and at the Royal Exchange. It was from this last address that the company conducted its turret clockmaking business. Both Airy and Denison had every confidence in Frederick Dent's capabilities; he had years of experience in the profession and it is he who is recorded in the inscription along the bedplate in the clock room as the maker, but Vulliamy saw this as an opportunity to exert his influence, and there followed some legal proceedings. The result of this action was to declare Dent's contract null and void. So, towards the end of 1853 there arose the ridiculous situation of Frederick Dent having almost completed the clock mechanism but being without a contract or any other means of obtaining payment for it. It is difficult to understand the purpose behind this action because if Dent was not to be allowed to finish the clock, who would? It certainly would not have been possible for him to pass the movement over to Vulliamy or to any other member of the Clockmakers' Company for completion, as they had stated on so many occasions that such a clock could never be built. One can only assume that the intention was to make things as difficult for Dent as possible. Despite this uncertainty, Dent continued to work on the mechanism, and fortunately the situation was resolved in the following year, 1854, when the original ruling was overturned and Dent was allowed to finish the clock. By this time the mechanism was virtually complete and, indeed, it was finished later that year. The contractual position had been resolved and the mechanism of the clock, which is over 15 feet in length and 5 tons in weight, was ready to undergo its extensive factory trials. These trials, carried out by staff from the Royal Observatory under the supervision of Airy and Denison, took place over a period of many months and were conducted with the utmost rigour.

In 1855, the Astronomer Royal notified the Chief Commissioner of his complete satisfaction with the mechanism and recommended that Dent be paid his fee. However, although the clock mechanism was now complete and had undergone all of its factory testing, there could be no question of installing it in the clock room as the tower, on which work had been started some twelve years previously, had not even risen to one half of its final height. Furthermore, before the mechanism could be put in place it would be necessary for the bells to be taken up the airshaft and installed above it in the belfry and the bells had yet to be cast. Consequently, there now arose the problem of having the completed clock mechanism and nowhere to keep it. However, this difficulty was soon overcome when Dent agreed to store it in his workshop at no cost, until the clock tower had been completed. This was a noble gesture on the part of Frederick Dent, especially when one bears in mind how unfairly he had been treated. The delay caused by the slow progress of the clock tower proved to be a blessing in disguise as it allowed Denison, who was never satisfied even with his most worthy efforts, to carry out many refinements in order to improve the accuracy of the clock.

Although the mechanism had easily maintained the standard required to meet the Astronomer Royal's specification while undergoing extensive testing in Dent's workshop, there remained one area of uncertainty – the clock's escapement. The escapement is the device which allows the power of the weights to escape to the hands under the control of the pendulum. It was believed that no design of escapement then in production would be capable of meeting the accuracy requirement for such a large clock. So Denison, who was by now concerned with designing the bells, took the opportunity to develop an improved form of escapement for the Great Clock. In Dent's workshop the mechanism had performed extremely well with Denison's first three-legged gravity escapement, but Denison was well aware of the difference between the clock's accuracy while running under controlled conditions in a stable environment and the likelihood of erratic behaviour once its heavy hands were exposed to ice, driving snow and wind. To further hone the performance, he tried a four-legged gravity escapement; this was a considerable improvement on its predecessor, but still he was not satisfied and continued his quest for perfection. After seemingly endless calculation he produced his masterpiece – the double three-legged gravity escapement – a truly ingenious piece of engineering. It was designed to be sensitive enough to maintain the required level of accuracy while preventing the effects of external pressures such as driving snow and wind on the hands from being reflected back to the pendulum and thus affecting the clock's timekeeping. So important was its invention that this escapement was considered to be one of the greatest advances in the science of horology; it was soon adopted as the standard and remains unaltered to this day, having been fitted to most large turret clocks throughout the world.

The great bell on which the Westminster clock would strike the hours was to be the largest ever cast in Britain. Sir Charles Barry's (he had been knighted in 1852) original plan called for an hour bell of 14 tons together with eight quarter bells of various sizes, but Denison had designed the mechanism to chime the quarters on just four bells and his reason for doing this will become apparent. At one time there were many foundries scattered throughout the length and breadth of the United Kingdom supplying bells for the numerous churches which were being built, but nowadays the few churches which are under construction are seldom provided with bells, so that the number of bell foundries has declined to such an extent that just two remain. As with the clock, tenders were invited from three founders for the manufacture of the bells – John Warner & Sons of Cripplegate, the Whitechapel Bell Foundry and John Taylor & Company of Loughborough. It is these last two that have survived, and they may both be justly proud of the many fine bells which they have produced. Like Vulliamy before him, George Mears of the Whitechapel Bell Foundry considered himself to be at the top of his craft and declined to tender in competition with anyone else. He also claimed that bells had been made at Whitechapel since before the reign of Queen Elizabeth I and, moreover, that his was the only firm in Britain with sufficient expertise to cast such a large bell. Warners were very keen to point out that they had recently commissioned two new large furnaces for their foundry at Norton, near Stockton on Tees, while Taylors insisted on receiving payment in advance. This was unacceptable to the Government and so the contract was let to Warners.

Fortunately, Denison had included campanology in his studies and as early as 1854 had been asked to act as referee for the design and construction of the bells. As the furnaces at Cripplegate were not capable of receiving such a large mould, it was decided that the great bell should be cast at Stockton on Tees, with Warners being responsible for its removal to London. The casting of the four smaller bells presented no problem to the Cripplegate foundry, but as Warners were unable to guarantee the note which would be sounded by the hour bell, their casting was delayed until this was known. Denison specified that the composition of all the bells should be twenty-two parts of copper to seven parts of tin. In the nineteenth century there was no way of gauging the exact mixture of the metals nor of measuring their temperature while molten, so the casting of such a large bell was a matter of some concern. Hitherto, no bell approaching 14 tons had been cast by a British foundry, the largest in Britain at the time being Great Peter, the bourdon bell of York Minster, which had been installed in 1845 and which weighed 10 tons. As this was to be the heaviest bell which had ever been made in Britain, it must have been with some trepidation that the mould was constructed and preparations were made for casting.

On 6 August 1856, the furnaces were fired and the great bell was cast. There were celebrations in the foundry when the mould was opened and the casting was seen to be complete, and this mood of celebration quickly spread to London where people had begun to wonder when they could expect to see the completion of the clock which they had been promised more than twenty years earlier. Now that the great bell had been cast, the difficulty which presented itself was that of having the bell in Stockton on Tees and the clock in London. It was not considered practical to attempt transporting the bell by road due to the poor condition of the nation's highways and the length of the journey involved, and as such a load would have undoubtedly exceeded the railways' loading gauge, some other method of transport had to be found. It was decided to convey the bell by sea, so it was taken to the nearby port of West Hartlepool from where it could continue its journey to London by ship. The bell was loaded on to a schooner, *The Wave*.

At this stage it became apparent that the bell was much heavier than its intended weight of 14 tons (in fact it weighed 16 tons), for it fell several inches from its support on to the deck, causing considerable damage and forcing the ship to put into dry dock for repair. It must have seemed that circumstances were conspiring against the bell for when the vessel finally put to sea she was caught in a heavy storm, and in London it was not long before rumours began to spread that both ship and bell had been lost. Fortunately, *The Wave* weathered the storm and there was great rejoicing in London on 21 October 1856 when she docked safely, bearing her valuable cargo undamaged. On arrival at the Port of London the bell was taken to the Cripplegate foundry where it underwent a further inspection. The bell was found to produce the note E; once this had been ascertained it was possible to cast the four quarter bells to harmonise.

When all the bells had been completed, the great bell was loaded on to a specially constructed carriage and vast crowds lined the route and cheered as it was drawn by sixteen white horses across Westminster Bridge and into New Palace Yard. The clock tower, which had been started some thirteen years previously in 1843, was still incomplete, so it was decided to suspend the bell from gallows which had been erected especially for the purpose near to the foot of the tower, where extensive testing could be carried out. Originally it had been intended to strike the bell with a 4cwt hammer, but when it was discovered that the bell exceeded its designed weight by 2 tons, a 6cwt hammer was brought into use as it was felt that a heavier hammer would be necessary to produce the maximum tone. The bell is believed to have carried the following inscription:

> Cast in the twentieth year of the reign of Her Majesty Queen Victoria, and in the year of Our Lord 1856; from the design of Edmund Beckett Denison Q.C. Sir Benjamin Hall M.P. Chief Commissioner of Works.

Sir Benjamin Hall had become Chief Commissioner of Works in 1855. His appointment proved extremely fortunate, as he was very sympathetic to the cause of the clock, and his charming personality resolved many tensions between Barry and Denison.

The bell underwent testing by being struck regularly throughout most of 1857 and was found to give an agreeable tone. Not unreasonably, the people of London must have supposed that, at last, after years of delay and uncertainty their great bell had arrived and would soon be raised to the belfry where it would sound the hours over Westminster. But it was not to be. On 17 October 1857, very nearly a year after its arrival in London, the bell cracked while being struck. A thorough examination revealed a crack about 4ft in length stretching up from the sound bow. Predictably, there was much controversy regarding the cause of the crack, Warners claiming that the fault lay with Denison for using the heavier hammer, while Denison claimed that the fault lay with Warners for manufacturing a poor casting. Whichever turned out to be the case, the result was the same – the bell would need to be broken up and recast.

3

Obstacles Overcome

Over a period of two days during February of the following year, 1858, a large iron ball weighing well over a ton was dropped repeatedly from a height of about 30ft on to the bell until it had been completely shattered and lay in small fragments. While the bell was undergoing demolition, a flaw in the metal was discovered just where the crack had started. Denison felt vindicated because this showed that the crack had most likely been caused by a poor casting, rather than by the use of the heavier hammer. In spite of this, Warners claimed that they could not be held responsible because the bell had been delivered the year previously and had undergone its many months of testing while being struck with a hammer far heavier than the one which they had recommended. The cracking of the bell was a devastating blow to the progress of the clock, and although the government felt that they had a claim, legal action against Warners could have dragged on for years, and even then may not have proved successful – and all the while Londoners were waiting for their clock. Hence the Office of Works asked Warners to put in a tender for recasting the bell, but this time to a higher specification than that which had been drawn up originally.

Meanwhile, at the Whitechapel Bell Foundry, Mears had been very sorry to have missed his opportunity to make the most famous bell in the world; now that it was to be recast, he reconsidered his position and asked to be allowed to tender. When the bids came in, Warner's estimate was reckoned to be excessive. Mears, however, quoted a very reasonable price and so a contract was let. The use of the Whitechapel Bell Foundry would also prove more convenient since the bell would be cast in London, thus avoiding the need to transport it once more from Teesside. By now, the public were becoming very impatient and must have wondered, after the ungainly departure of Big Ben I, if they would ever see the clock which they had been promised so many years earlier. Their feelings were summed up very aptly in this little rhyme which became very popular in London about that time:

> Poor Mr Warner is put in a corner
> For making a bad Big Ben
> Good Mr Mears, or so it appears
> Will make us a new one, but when?

In fact, Mears wasted no time in setting to work. The broken pieces of the earlier bell were loaded into carts and taken to Whitechapel. The mould was prepared right away, and benefiting from his competitor's earlier experience, Mears made sure that the dimensions were exactly as shown on Denison's specification.

On 10 April 1858 the furnaces were fired and, once again, the great bell was cast. When the metal had been allowed to cool and the mould was opened, the casting was seen to be complete and there were celebrations in the foundry, although these may well have been more cautious than those which had been held on the earlier occasion at Stockton on Tees. The bell was found to weigh just over 13½ tons, being some 2 tons lighter than its predecessor. It also sounded the note E as intended, which was very fortunate as the quarter bells had now been cast to harmonise. The bell underwent extensive tests before being loaded on to a carriage and once more crowds lined the route and cheered as it was drawn by sixteen horses, this time from Whitechapel through the streets of London and into New Palace Yard. The bell glistened in the brilliant sunshine. (It may have been coated with a layer of varnish which had the effect not only of enhancing its appearance but also of concealing a number of minor defects and blemishes.)

The clock tower, although well advanced, was still not ready to receive the bells, so the new bell was suspended from the very same gallows which had been used to test the earlier one. It was struck with the same 6cwt hammer which had been used for testing the old bell, and according to the reports of the time the new bell was considered to sound a much improved and superior tone. This new bell, which we shall call Big Ben II and which has since become so familiar, particularly to Londoners, has the Royal Coat of Arms on one side and the portcullis of the Palace of Westminster on the other. It carries the following inscription around the skirt in letters of iron:

The bell weighing 13 tons 10 cwt 3 qrs 15 lbs was cast by George Mears of Whitechapel for the clock of the Houses of Parliament under the direction of Edmund Beckett Denison Q C in the twenty-first year of the reign of Queen Victoria and in the year of Our Lord MDCCCLVIII.

Towards the late summer of 1858, work on the clock tower had progressed sufficiently to allow the fitting of the bells. The four quarter bells, which had been cast at Warner's Cripplegate foundry in London's East End, were very large for quarter bells in the nineteenth century and raising them all to the belfry above the clock room was to be a considerable task. The bells were lifted individually by means of a hand-driven winch over a period of a few days, and after they had been hoisted and secured in position, one in each corner of the belfry, they were ready to be joined by the hour bell. The raising of the great bell was to be an altogether different matter. The bell was, at the time, the heaviest in the British Isles – and by quite some margin. The task of lifting it to the belfry some 200ft above ground level appears not to have been given a great deal of thought when the shaft, through which the bell would need to be raised, was designed, since this duct was just 8ft 6in wide. Had the bell been made to the conventional shape, it would have been too large to pass through the shaft, so the ingenious Denison had designed it to be 7ft 6in in height and 9ft in diameter. It would then be possible to turn the great bell on its side and encase it within a cradle prior to drawing it up the shaft and into the belfry. The bell was duly turned on its side and a wooden cradle constructed around it. Then, on 12 October 1858, the bell was winched very slowly through the airshaft. The task was extremely laborious and took the teams of men, working in relays, some days to complete. Eventually the bell was delivered safely into the belfry and secured to the massive iron girders. At last Big Ben was in position and there must have been many a sigh of relief from the men who has striven so hard to complete such a heavy and yet such a delicate operation. With the bells in place, it was now possible to hoist the mechanism up, through the airshaft and into the clock room, an exacting task which was carried out with the utmost care.

Assembly of the clock took place during the early months of 1859. The driveshafts which extend from the mechanism to the four dials and which turn the hands were fitted, and the weights which provide the energy to drive the clock and to sound the bells were attached to the massive drums by means of steel cables. The mechanism comprises three 'trains', each of which is powered by a heavy weight. The going train is the heart of the clock and does exactly what its name implies – it keeps the clock going by driving the hands and controlling the operation of the other two trains which sound the bells. It is the smallest of the three trains and is powered by a 5cwt cast iron weight. The other trains are much larger as they need to provide sufficient energy to lift the heavy bell hammers many times a day. The striking train, which sounds the hours, is powered by a 1-ton weight while the chiming train, which sounds the quarters, is powered by an even larger 1¼-ton weight. The two flyfans, which regulate the speed of chiming and striking, were installed high above the mechanism. Each consists of two sheets of metal, mounted edge on, to either side of a vertical metal shaft extending upwards from the mechanism. When the bells are sounding the shaft revolves and it is the flyfan, acting like an airbrake, which controls the tempo of the bells and makes for such even spacing between the strokes. It is the conventional practice in clockmaking to mount the flyfans close to the mechanism on horizontal shafts but due to poor relations between Barry and Denison insufficient space had been provided behind the clock frame to allow for this and the only solution was to take the shafts upwards, almost to the ceiling. This amendment to the design had the most unfortunate consequences as it proved to be the cause of the great disaster which was to follow more than a century later. The mechanism had, of course, been completed five years previously and bears the following inscription along both the front and the back girders of the clock frame in letters of cast iron:

THIS CLOCK WAS MADE IN THE YEAR OF OUR LORD 1854 BY FREDERICK DENT, OF THE STRAND AND THE ROYAL EXCHANGE, CLOCKMAKER TO THE QUEEN, FROM THE DESIGNS OF EDMUND BECKETT DENISON Q.C.

When the installation had been completed, just below the inscription at the front was added a small plate which records: 'FIXED HERE 1859'.

The faces of the clock are just as well known as the bells. With the tower virtually complete, it was possible to instal the dials, which are the work of Pugin, and as a consequence are most beautifully designed. In his original plan, Barry had specified that each face should be 30ft in diameter; in fact, Pugin reduced this to 23ft and, as a result, the faces are in the most perfect proportion to the tower. Each dial incorporates an exquisite tracery containing 312 pieces of opal glass. The figures are of particular interest, being Roman numerals but set in Pugin Gothic script. A notable departure from the usual practice is the use of IV at the four o'clock marking. Traditionally, clockmakers have favoured the use of IIII, although how this came about is something of a mystery. The convention may have had its origins in an incident said to have occurred in France towards the end of the fourteenth century. King Charles V had commissioned a clock for the royal palace (now the Palais de Justice) in Paris from the German clockmaker Heinrich von Wieck, who was known in France as Henri de Vic. When the clock, which had taken some years to construct, was received, the king objected to the use of the figure IV on the dial. De Vic protested that both forms of the numeral had been in use during ancient times, but the king told him to take the clock away and 'correct' it. Since that time the use of IIII on clock faces has been adopted almost universally. It is not known why this tradition was not followed in the case of the Westminster Clock – it may have been no more than lack of communication between architect and clockmaker. Whatever the reason, whether mistaken or intended, it is one of those curiosities which go, perhaps, just a little way to make the clock so special. Of course, one may come across other examples of the figure IV in the four o'clock position, but no doubt these clocks have their own story. It must be remembered that this was to be a noble and elegant clock, indeed the finest ever constructed, and no effort was spared to ensure that its appearance would befit its status. To complete the ornamentation, a considerable amount of gilding was applied to the metalwork of the spire and the top finial, which is set in the form of a ball and a shower of stars. Under each face in letters of gold was placed the following Latin inscription: 'Domine Salvam fac Reginam nostram Victoriam primam', which translates as: O Lord, save our Queen Victoria I. It is interesting to note that the inscription refers to Victoria as *the first* – this designation has never been in general use and one wonders if there could ever be another. The clock was to strike the hours over Victorian London for more than forty years.

The overall effect of the faces is extremely pleasing, especially when the gilding is caught in gentle sunlight. At night, the dials are illuminated so that the time may be read from a considerable distance. Originally lighting was provided by gas jets, but it was replaced by electricity in the early twentieth century. At this point, mention may be made of the lantern which shines out from above the dials, although it was not installed until many years after the clock had been completed. This is the Ayrton Light; situated above the belfry about 250ft from ground level it is illuminated when either House is sitting after dark. The feature was the brainchild of Acton Ayrton, MP and Chief Commissioner of Works in the 1870s, but it did not come into operation until 1885. When the Union flag, flown from the Victoria Tower every day while Parliament is sitting, is lowered at sunset, if the session is still in progress, the Ayrton Light is lit. It is extinguished when the House rises. The original light was only visible from certain directions, but the present light, installed in 1892, has the advantage that it can be seen from every angle. This light, too, was originally powered by gas, but has been electrically operated since the early years of the twentieth century.

At last, by the spring of 1859, almost twenty-five years after the fire that had destroyed the ancient Palace of Westminster, the clock was nearly complete. All that remained was to fit the hands, and the clock would be ready for service – or would it? The hands were fitted and the clock was started experimentally but, alas, it would not go even for so much as an hour, no matter what adjustments were made. Denison's enemies smelled blood, and there were some venomous exchanges in *The Times*. It was soon discovered that the cause of the trouble lay with the weight of the hands. They had been designed by Barry and were fashioned into an elegant Gothic design in cast iron. They were far too heavy for the mechanism to drive so that the clock came to a standstill as the minute hand approached the hour. Barry designed a new set of 'lightweight' hands, this time from hollow gunmetal. In fact, these hands were so light that Barry was forced to strengthen them by securing them to heavy copper backing plates. Had he not done this, the hands would probably have blown away during the first

storm. They were now almost as heavy as the
original cast iron hands which had been rejected
and, of course, as the minute hand reached the
vertical, the mechanism could not hold it and it
fell over by a minute or two under its own weight.
All this was too much for the exasperated Denison,
who, despairing of the whole affair, designed a
new set of minute hands and had them made from
hollow copper. These were found to be entirely
satisfactory. As the slower speed of rotation made
the additional weight less important, it was
decided to retain the gunmetal hour hands,
together with their needlessly heavy copper
backing plates. Thus the final design incorporated
the second (Barry's) set of gunmetal hour hands
and the third (Denison's) set of copper minute
hands. This combination worked perfectly, and
has done so ever since, for it is the arrangement
which we see today. With the problem of the
hands resolved, the clock was now complete.

The very best in horological science and
engineering had produced a magnificent clock,
indeed not only a clock which represented the
very pinnacle of turret clockmaking and which
would set the standard for all others, but also a
clock which the majority of makers believed could
never have been produced. So long had the Great
Clock taken to arrive, after all its countless trials
and setbacks, that some of those who had been
involved in its planning and construction did not
live to see it strike its first hour. Augustus Welby

Pugin, whose work on the dials is such a joy to behold, seemed to dwell on the border between genius and insanity and died in 1852 at the age of forty in a sanatorium; while Edward Dent, who had been awarded the contract to build the clock, died in the following year, 1853. Louis Vulliamy, who had maintained so vehemently that the clock would never be built, died in 1854. Frederick Dent, who completed the mechanism, did live to see the clock completed, but only just – he died in 1860. Although Sir Charles Barry lived to see Big Ben come into service, he never had the pleasure of beholding his masterpiece as he, too, passed away in 1860, just a short time before the completion of the new Houses of Parliament which are considered to be the greatest monument to his genius. Sir Benjamin Hall, whose quiet diplomacy had done so much to further the progress of the clock, and whose name will forever be associated with the great bell, died in 1867, having become Lord Llanover. Both George Airy and Edmund Beckett Denison went on to enjoy very long lives, each surviving until his ninetieth year. Airy was knighted at the age of seventy-one, while Denison was made Sir Edmund Beckett at the age of fifty-eight in 1874, eventually becoming Lord Grimthorpe in 1886 when he was seventy. The Grimthorpe motto is very appropriate: PRODESSE CIVIBUS, 'to benefit my fellow citizens', something which Edmund Beckett Denison must have been very proud to have done, for despite his aggressive manner and general unpopularity, Denison was the brains behind the machine; it was entirely due to his scientific knowledge, tireless enthusiasm and determination that the Great Clock was ever brought into being. Gradually Denison had taken over the project until he was working almost single-handedly and with virtually sole responsibility. Promising the Great Clock was one thing but finding someone who could build it was quite another, as the commissioners had discovered very early on. Denison, who cared little for other people's feelings and even less for vested interests, had designed a dream clock, and the dream was about to come true. A final period of testing during the late spring of 1859 showed the mechanism to be operating perfectly and so, after years of delay and frustration, at last the Great Clock of the Royal Palace of Westminster was ready to commence duties as the nation's timekeeper.

4

The First Tick – then Trouble

The clock was started officially, as far as can be reasonably ascertained, on Tuesday 31 May 1859, this date selected to coincide with the Opening of Parliament. It was not a formal occasion as there appears to have been little or no attendant ceremony. Although this lack of publicity might be considered 'low key' today, it is likely that Denison and Dent deliberately eschewed the monotony of a succession of lengthy speeches made by pompous officials, some of whom would probably have had no more than a tenuous connection with the clock, preferring to let events take their course quietly. It was a proud day for London. After the seemingly endless delays and disappointments the sight of the clock in place on the tower must have appeared too good to be true – and, indeed, as history has shown so very often, if things seem that way, they usually are.

Even at this stage, hands had been fitted to only two of the dials, but it was not long before the remaining sets were in place and the clock was displaying the time on all four faces, and its performance was found to be every bit as accurate as had been promised. But the clock was still silent and it was not until 11 July that the great bell was brought into service and Big Ben started to strike the hours. This was the day Londoners had been waiting for. The tone of the bell proved to be popular with the public, but not with all Members of Parliament, some of whom took it upon themselves to complain that it was too loud. Nevertheless, for the very first time, the people had been provided with an audible signal which denoted the exact hour. However, because of weaknesses in the floor carrying the cranks and levers which link the chiming mechanism to its bell hammers, it was not possible to introduce the quarter bells on the same day; in fact, almost another two months were to elapse before 7 September, when the four bells started chiming the quarters and the clock was complete with the bells sounding their beautiful music, which has become part of Britain's heritage. Dent, Denison and Airy had triumphed and the king of clocks, which many supposed could never have been built had commenced his reign sounding the hours not only over the Palace of Westminster, but also far beyond. All those who had been involved in the planning and construction no doubt looked back with feelings of great pride and satisfaction at what had been achieved; regrettably, this happy state of affairs was to last for just a few short weeks during the early autumn of 1859, for on 1 October the unthinkable happened – the great bell cracked.

On Monday 3 October *The Times* carried the following report:

THE BELL OF WESTMINSTER

On Saturday the great bell of Westminster sounded for the last time, and while in the very act of striking Big Ben became dumb for ever. At the present moment the bell is even more hopelessly cracked than its ill-fated predecessor, and like him, too, must be broken up and recast before the great clock of the metropolis can again record the flight of time. Recasting is a word which is soon said; but such a weary deal has to be done before Ben's mutilated fragments find their way to the melting pot, and still more before the renovated mass is again restored to its lofty dwelling, that, even taking a sanguine view of things, we think at the least a clear twelve-month must elapse before the voice of the great bell can again be heard booming over the great province of houses in which it is to regulate the laws of time. The first bell was cast by the Messrs Warner, and on trial proved so much heavier than was expected that a clapper of nearly double the weight than originally intended had to be used to elicit the sound. Under the infliction of repeated trials the bell broke in Palace-yard, and most fortunately before it had been raised to its resting place amid the iron beams and girders of the bell-chamber in the

BIG BEN

summit of the clock-tower. It was accordingly broken up and recast, showing, during the first-named process, that the first casting had been a failure. To Messrs Mears of Whitechapel the recasting of the second bell was entrusted, Messrs Warner declining to undertake it on the terms offered by the Board of Works. The second bell which has just cracked was a magnificent casting. Its weight, size, and tone were exactly what was required, and Mr Denison most properly certified to the completeness of the largest and finest bell ever cast in England. This was, as usual, tested, and at last after considerable delay and trouble hoisted to its place above the clock-room. The peculiar iron framework from which Big Ben and the quarter chimes were to hang has been so repeatedly described in these columns that a repetition now would be almost useless. It will suffice to say, therefore, that it was amply strong enough for bells hung as they usually are hung, that is swinging to a certain extent free and yielding to the stroke of the hammer. This mode, however, was not the one adopted, and, contrary to the experience of all bell-hangers from time immemorial, Big Ben was firmly bolted to the beam from which he hung and made as rigid as the walls of the tower itself. Thus fixed, his tone was tried; the clapper was swung to its full extent. The result, as may easily be anticipated, was that the rigid bell acted like a gigantic lever upon the bell frame, which worked dangerously, while it was evident that the tone of the bell itself was seriously impaired by the rigidity of its fastenings, which of course prevented much of the vibration. Both these facts were clearly pointed out in the account of the trial of the bell which appeared in this journal. So matters dragged on, the clock was not going, the bell-frame was not fastened. Through the columns of *The Times* public attention was directed to the delay, but with very little result, beyond eliciting the usual amount of denial, complaint, and flat contradiction from all concerned in the matter in any way or form. Parliamentary papers were moved for and produced, in the interest of all the great contending parties, but they only made bad worse, as none contained the whole truth, while some contained no truth at all. At last, when it is not too much to say the public were disgusted with the whole affair, and weary of the mismanagement and waste of money which each fresh enquiry disclosed, the clock at length was fixed, and Big Ben began to number hours, though his own, as it seems, were of the shortest. . . . The only remedy now left is to remove the clock, get down the bell, break it up and recast it for the third time, prove it, get it up the tower again, and refix the clock under it as soon as may be. If these six operations average, on the whole, less than three months to each, why the work will be very quickly done. An old adage tells us the fate of the best broth with too many cooks to prepare it. In the name of common prudence let the contract for the next bell be given to some one of our eminent bell founders who have passed their lives and realized fortunes in the manufacture of bells of all kinds. Let such a man be told what is wanted, and let him be responsible that it is forthcoming. We may then hope to have a bell which will be a pride instead of a grievance to the public mind.

The clock had been operating in its originally intended form for less than a month. As usual, the long-suffering British public had been very patient. At the laying of the foundation stone in 1843 they had expected that the clock would be complete within a few years, certainly before the end of the decade. Instead, they had endured countless delays and arguments and now, sixteen years later, after sounding the hours for a few glorious weeks, the clock was again silent. What had gone wrong, and who was to blame?

A close inspection of the bell confirmed the existence of a crack very nearly 1ft long and running vertically from the sound bow. This time, there was a much greater controversy regarding the cause of the crack. George Mears of the Whitechapel Bell Foundry blamed Denison for continuing to use the heavier hammer, while Denison laid the blame squarely on the foundry for manufacturing a poor casting – much the same situation as on the first occasion. Mears, however, was not prepared to concede that the bell was defective and took out a libel action against Denison. It is not known why Denison had not reverted to the 4cwt hammer for the new bell, which was much closer to the original weight specification. He may have considered that the 6cwt hammer gave a better tone. Eventually, it was arranged for some samples to be removed from the bell for chemical analysis. This revealed a poor mixture of the metals: in the area of the crack there was a deficiency of copper and this meant that the metal would be very brittle just where the hammer strikes the bell. Once again, Denison had been vindicated: for almost certainly it had been shown that it was the poor casting that had caused the bell to crack. On two counts the report in *The Times* had not been entirely correct; first, the original hour bell was the largest to have been cast in England; but, more relevantly, the crack in the new bell was considerably smaller than that in the earlier one. Although this time the crack was smaller, the problem it presented was very much larger.

When the original bell had cracked it was still in New Palace Yard and was easily accessible; now, the clock was complete and Big Ben II had been raised to the belfry, 200ft above street level. The debate raged as to how to find a solution. For Denison, the perfectionist, there was, of course, just one answer: break up and recast the bell. Not surprisingly, everybody else who was involved recoiled in horror at the sheer magnitude of the task which this would have entailed. To recast the bell it would have been necessary to remove the mechanism from the clock room immediately below, as it bridges the shaft through which the bell would have to be lowered. Also, the drive-shafts would have had to be dismantled and the pulleys and weights removed, all of which had been positioned so meticulously and aligned with such care. Furthermore, the shaft would need to be relined with timber and the masonry walls cut in order to permit the removal of the bell from the base of the tower. Not only that, but the clock would have been out of action during the time it took to make a new casting. And then, of course, there would be the difficulty of raising the new bell to the top of the tower, reassembling the mechanism in the clock room immediately beneath it, refixing the weights and pulleys and realigning the driveshafts before testing and starting the clock once more. Another point to be considered was that now the clock was being relied upon by Parliament, and as there could be no telling how long the task might take, it could have been very difficult to obtain authority for the work to proceed – to say nothing of the expense, which would have been considerable. In view of all these difficulties, it is quite understandable that the commissioners considered themselves obliged to look for other ways in which to solve the problem. After all, unlike the crack in Big Ben I which was 4ft long, this crack was just under 1ft long; surely there must be an easier solution?

Of the two clock referees, there was little point in consulting Denison as, since the day it cracked, he maintained that the bell was defective and should be recast. So the commissioners turned to Airy for advice on how to remedy the situation. Airy was a practical scientist and, after considering the matter thoroughly, he put forward some simple but effective suggestions: first, that the bell be turned by a quarter so that the hammer would strike a different spot; second, that the weight of the hammer be reduced by about one third in order to lessen the impact upon the bell; and, third, that a sturdy platform be constructed beneath the bell to protect the tower in the event that the bell should be broken further or shatter completely. Compared with the alternative, these recommendations involved little disruption and as they were thought to provide the best possible solution, they were readily accepted by the commissioners.

Big Ben had cracked in October 1859 since when the clock had been silent, and it was by no means certain when the great bell would be striking the hours once more. As we saw from the newspaper report, some believed that it was damaged to such an extent that it would never sound again. Although it was unlikely that Big Ben would be available for service in the immediate future, Airy considered it desirable that striking be restored as

soon as possible, and in June 1860 he suggested
that the striking mechanism be modified to sound
the hours on the largest of the quarter bells (B)
which gives the lowest tone, while Big Ben was
out of action. He proposed that the quarters should
be chimed on the smallest two bells (G sharp and
F sharp), the one remaining bell being taken out of
use altogether. The higher note would be chimed
first and the interval sounded once for quarter
past, twice for half past and so on, being followed
on the hour by the strike. This arrangement is
known as the 'ting tang' or 'ding dong' chime and
it is to be found fairly commonly in turret clocks,
the best known example being that at St Paul's
Cathedral. Now, imagine the Westminster 'quarter
past' chime in your mind's ear. When the bells
were designed, they were intended to sound the
following notes: G sharp, F sharp, E and B, respectively. Around this time, however, there appear
to have arisen differing views regarding the notes
which were sounded by the bells and it was
decided to obtain the opinion of a respected
musician. James Furle, organist at the nearby
Westminster Abbey was approached and asked to
determine the note played by each bell. Furle had
the bells sounded several times, and gave the notes
as A, G, F and C, that is to say, one semitone
higher than had been supposed, in each case. Of
course, since sound recording was still unknown
in the middle of the nineteenth century, there was
no way of 'preserving' the notes for replaying later

and any assessment had to be made on the spot. But Furle had given the wrong notes for the chimes. They are, in fact, G sharp, F sharp, E and B, as intended originally, with the hour bell also striking E but one octave below the quarter bell.

Furle disliked the monotony of the temporary chimes which Airy had proposed and suggested something a little more adventurous, of his own invention. Again the hour would be sounded by the largest of the quarter bells which gives the note B, but the three remaining bells would be chimed in various combinations to denote the quarter hours, two notes being played at quarter past (G sharp and E), four at half past (E, F sharp, G sharp and E), six at quarter to (G sharp, E, F sharp, G sharp, F sharp and E) and eight (E, G sharp, F sharp, E, F sharp, G sharp, F sharp and E) preceding the strokes on the hour. Airy raised no objection to this scheme and it appears to have been adopted sometime during the summer of 1860.

With the other bells sounding once again, attention could be given to turning Big Ben. First, a small slot of metal was cut out of the sound bow just at the lower end of the crack in order to prevent it from developing further, and then the bell was turned through about 90 degrees. Next, a new hammer weighing 4cwt was fitted in place of the heavier one and, lastly, the very substantial timber platform was built under the great bell. This new arrangement was found to provide an agreeable tone and it has remained in place ever since.

Although the continual striking of the bell has produced some flattening of the surface, the crack has not extended, nor has it ever been found necessary to turn the bell again – it remains in exactly the same position today. The original hammer has been retained and may be seen by visitors to the clock tower, where it is displayed. It bears the following notice:

BIG BEN HAMMER

———

THIS IS THE ORIGINAL HAMMER USED
FOR STRIKING BIG BEN IN 1859. IT
WEIGHS 6½ CWTS & WAS FOUND
TO BE TOO HEAVY. IN 1862 IT WAS
REPLACED BY THE PRESENT ONE OF 4 CWTS

In 1862, with the great bell having been turned and ready to sound the hours once more, the original chimes were brought back into play and the music of the bells has remained the same ever since, just as we hear it today. To be precise, the tuning of the bells is probably not *exactly* their intended notes; they are not 'perfect pitch' and all deviate, very slightly, from the notes which they are supposed to sound, but this serves to make them recognisable instantly, and of course above all it is the crack which gives Big Ben its individual and unmistakable tone. Despite what had been reported in *The Times* after it had cracked, Denison was by no means satisfied with the bell. He now regarded it as a thoroughly bad casting and, as usual, he was not afraid to say so. Apart from revealing the extent of the crack, the original inspection had also brought to light a number of flaws in the metal, all of which had been very skilfully concealed by filling them with a mixture of bell dust and cement. Denison contended that the bell would never have been accepted at all if these defects had not been deliberately concealed and he never deviated from his opinion that it should be broken up and recast. Others paid little attention to his call for another recasting and, in any event, Denison's connection with the clock had officially come to an end on its completion. With its initial troubles now behind it, the clock could look forward to giving very many years of excellent service over London.

In 1863, the electromagnetic link was established with the Royal Observatory at Greenwich for the purpose of comparing the accuracy of the Great Clock with Greenwich Mean Time, twice a day. This was one of Airy's original fifteen conditions and it was achieved by laying a special telegraph line between the clock and the observatory, an electric signal then being transmitted from contacts behind the bronze dial on the mechanism in the clock room. It was soon discovered that the clock's performance was well within the limits which had been set by the

Astronomer Royal's specification. The new clock was proving to be very useful, not only to Parliament where the timing of debates is so important, but also to the general population of London. In the mid nineteenth century, more than fifty years before the advent of broadcasting and radio time signals, the new clock made the exact time generally available. Today, if a quartz wristwatch is left to run for a year, it is unlikely to vary by more than a minute from the time, but in the 1860s of course, such technology lay more than a century in the future and, as clockwork watches are liable to very erratic running, the clock provided a valuable and much appreciated service. Because sound travels rather slowly (about 1 mile in 5 seconds), maps of London produced around this time often depicted circles centred on Westminster, and printed at intervals of one second, which allowed the user to compensate for the effect of 'sound time', according to his distance from the clock tower. Although the London of Victorian times resounded to the echoes of horse carriages and the cries of street traders, being before the advent of motor traffic it was probably still quieter than it is today and the sound of the bells would have been heard clearly, possibly for some miles under good conditions. Nowadays, unfortunately, the bells can be drowned by the constant passing of vehicles, even when they are listened to at quite close range. As has already been explained, in 1880 the government passed the Definition of Time Act which established Greenwich Mean Time as the standard for the British Isles and, since then, all clocks in the United Kingdom have been set to Greenwich time.

A further development came about in October 1884 when an inter-governmental conference was held in Washington for the purpose of considering a treaty for the establishment of a prime meridian, from which all longitudes would be reckoned. Because there had been more than two hundred years of continuous astronomical observation carried out at the Royal Observatory, and since the majority of navigational charts were based on Greenwich, that meridian seemed an obvious choice and indeed it was adopted in the resulting Prime Meridian Treaty. Summer Time came in much later, the Daylight Saving Act being introduced as a wartime measure in 1916: British Summer Time, one hour ahead of GMT, is usually in operation from March until October.

In the 1860s, reflecting on the completion of the immense task which had been involved in the construction of the Great Clock, Denison had written:

So ends the history of the clock up to the present time, having already seen the deaths of the three clockmakers, the architect, and two Commissioners of Works, whose names are involved in it. What further vicissitudes it may have to go through, I cannot pretend to guess, save as the future may be divined from the past. Too many people have had to be disappointed, defeated and exposed in getting it there, for its existence to be easily forgiven, or for any of its occasional failures, such as all machines are liable to, not to be magnified into radical defects if possible. Meanwhile, anyone who has really accurate means of judging can observe that this huge cast iron machine, which has to drive through all weathers such a weight of hands as no other clock in the world, keeps better time than the best public clock you can find of the common size. And it should never be forgotten that the designer and supporters of the rival plan confessed that they could do no such things, and derided the possibility of making a clock of this size keep accurate time at all.

Since we can never know exactly how the great bell sounded originally, the clock as it is known today may be said to date from the resumption of striking Big Ben in 1862. From time to time there have been proposals to recast not only Big Ben but also the four quarter bells to modern standards, and it is probably true that to do so would make for an improved tone, for today it is possible to tune bells electronically. But quite apart from the scale of the operation which would be involved, the considerable and long-founded sentimental attachment to the distinctive sound means that this is very unlikely ever to be attempted. After all, the present system has worked extremely well for almost one hundred and fifty years and continues to do so.

This, then, is how the Great Clock came to Westminster and how the bell survived a major disaster just weeks after being brought into use. After such a devastating setback when many had presumed that the bell would never sound again, Big Ben had overcome the almost impossible odds and triumphed. Behind the clock were many years of bitter arguments and countless delays, ahead lay more than a century of practically unfailing service which was to be broken by the great catastrophe of 1976 when metal fatigue tore much of the mechanism apart and left the chimes silent for many months. During this time the 'national timekeeper at Westminster', as the Board of Works had decreed as early as 1846 that clock should be, was to become not only the symbol of Great Britain, but also the most celebrated timepiece in the world.

5

The Name of the Bell and the Music of the Chimes

Big Ben is the great bell on which the clock strikes the hours. Originally this name was given just to the bell but over the years popular usage has come to include not only the great bell but also the chimes, the clock tower, the mechanism and even the surrounding area. To be pedantic, the clock is the Great Clock of the Royal Palace of Westminster, which definition serves to distinguish it from the numerous other clocks located within the palace, should such a distinction ever be considered necessary, and even for the bell, Big Ben is a nickname; today nobody can be sure how it came to be adopted.

Since time immemorial, bells have been given names. Every large bell needs a name; for example Great Paul, the bourdon bell of St Paul's Cathedral and the heaviest bell in Britain, is named after the saint to whom that church has been dedicated, as is Great Peter, the bourdon bell of York Minster; the bell of Westminster was to be no exception. A name had to be chosen which would befit its status. Any official records are thought to have disappeared long ago and although sources vary it seems that the original proposal was to call the bell either Victoria or possibly Royal Victoria in honour of Her Majesty; St Stephen or even Great Stephen were also suggested, after the chapel of St Stephen situated within the Palace of Westminster, the crypt of which, along with Westminster Hall, was saved from the fire in 1834.

Incidentally, Victoria is the name which has been given to one of the palace's three towers. The Victoria Tower, the tallest of the three, rises elegantly to 323ft over the Royal Entrance to the House of Lords at the southern end of the palace and is just 7ft taller than the clock tower, which stands at 316ft at the northern end. The Central Tower, so beautifully fashioned by Barry to balance the other two, is much lower, just reaching 300ft and is situated roughly midway between them, not far from St Stephen's Entrance. Tradition has it that St Stephen's Chapel was founded in the twelfth century by King Stephen. The original Norman building was pulled down in 1292 and from 1547 the chamber was used by the Commons. It was enlarged during the early part of the nineteenth century and the area is now known as St Stephen's Hall. Although this name is never used in connection with the clock or the bell nowadays, it is interesting to recall that when the present bell cracked in October 1859, the *Daily Telegraph* reported: 'The great bell of St Stephen's tolled his last on Saturday afternoon, "Big Ben" like his predecessor, is cracked and his doleful E natural will never again be heard booming over the metropolis.' As we know now, very fortunately this prediction was not to be fulfilled.

The Central Tower is quite different from the others, which are square in section. It surmounts the Octagon Hall which is some 60ft in diameter and ends in a slender and ornate spire which is not so conspicuous as the two larger towers, and can only be seen well from across the river. The Octagon Hall is the centre of the building and marks the division between the House of Commons and the House of Lords. At one time there had also been a proposal to name the northern tower the Albert Tower, after the Prince Consort, but this idea seems to have fallen by the wayside because it has always been known quite simply as the clock tower.

George Mears of the Whitechapel Bell Foundry was said to be keen to dedicate his most famous casting to Queen Victoria, but if this were the case the name was soon forgotten in favour of Big Ben. There is a similarity here with the thirteenth-century bell which was christened after the king as Edward of Westminster but which has been known ever since as Great Tom.

Throughout the years the name of Big Ben has elicited considerable fascination and there are two theories as to how the bell came to be named. When the original bell was delivered in 1856, it was mounted on gallows in New Palace Yard prior to being tested for almost a year before shattering under the relentless blows inflicted by the continual use of the 6cwt hammer. The largest bell ever cast in the British Isles, at almost 16 tons it would have appeared colossal. As mentioned already it is believed to have been inscribed with the name of 'Sir Benjamin Hall MP Chief Commissioner of Works'. It has been suggested that some of the workmen responsible for setting up the bell for testing, being impressed with its great size and seeing the name Benjamin on the inscription decided to call it Big Ben.

There is also the better-known story of how, one hot afternoon, probably in the summer of 1857, a special sitting was held in the Commons for the purpose of deciding upon a name for the bell. This appears to have run into a lengthy session, because the debate had been in progress for some time and Members were becoming increasingly weary of the whole affair, when Sir Benjamin Hall, MP for Marylebone and Chief Commissioner of Works, launched into a lengthy discourse on behalf of the government. Sir Benjamin was very popular with both sides of the House, being a good humoured, jovial character, and of con-siderable proportions, standing some 6ft 4in and having a rather large girth. He was known affectionately as 'Big Ben'. The tale relates that as the Chief Commissioner was speaking, a back bencher, longing to see the end of the debate, interrupted to say 'Why not call it Big Ben?' The

House erupted with much hearty laughter and the name stuck. Unfortunately, there is no mention of this in *Hansard*, so we shall never know if it is any more than an anecdote.

There is also the possibility, if rather less likely, that the bell was named after Benjamin Caunt, a heavyweight prizefighter who was very popular at that time. At one stage he weighed 17 stone, and he too had also earned the nickname 'Big Ben'. A contemporary print described him as 'the distinguished knight of the bare-knuckled prize ring'. He had been the champion of England in 1841 at the age of twenty-five and he retired from boxing shortly after the second bell cracked, having despatched many formidable opponents during a long and notable career. At one time he was also the publican of a hostelry in the East End of London. Whichever is the case, the bell has certainly become far more famous than either of these men.

The considered view is that the bell was named after Sir Benjamin Hall, the Chief Commissioner of Works, and if this is the case it is very fitting as he had the gift of quiet diplomacy and his warm genial personality and gentle power of persuasion did much to smooth relations between the clockmaker and the architect during difficult times and to further the progress of the clock. Interestingly, the inscription on the present, second 'Big Ben' does not show the name of the Chief Commissioner. Although Sir Benjamin Hall had signed the order for the bell, ironically by the time it was cast in April 1858, he was no longer Chief Commissioner of Works, having been succeeded in that post two months earlier by Lord John Manners, Duke of Rutland. During the course of researching this book, I came across some correspondence in *The Times* from a Miss Maxwell Frazer who had written a biography of Sir Benjamin Hall. In the course of so doing she had contacted Major John Berrington, a great-nephew of Hall. Berrington's father had been Hall's private secretary at the time the (first) bell was cast and he had told Berrington that the bell had been named after Hall, but in committee, rather than in the Commons. If this were correct, it would explain why there is no reference in *Hansard*.

So what do we know about the man after whom the great bell is most likely to have been named? Benjamin Hall was born in 1802. He was educated at Westminster School in London and matriculated at Oxford in 1820, although without taking a degree. He entered Parliament in 1831 as the Member for Monmouth and in 1837 was returned as the Member for Marylebone, a seat which he was to hold for the next twenty-two years. He inherited a baronetcy in 1838. He was interested in ecclesiastical matters and campaigned in Parliament for the right of the Welsh to have church services conducted in their own tongue. He became President of the General Board of Health in 1854, being promoted to Chief Commissioner of Works in

July 1855 and holding that position until February 1858. Upon resigning his seat in the Commons in June 1859 he was elevated to the peerage as Baron Llanover of Llanover and Abercarn in the county of Monmouth. Finally, in 1861, he became Lord Lieutenant of Monmouthshire. He died in 1867. Today, few of us will have heard of Sir Benjamin Hall, but the name of Big Ben for the bell seems to have caught on immediately, even though Sir Benjamin had resigned from the Commons during the month before the Great Clock struck its first hour. The name was spread throughout the kingdom by the newspapers, and now, mainly through the medium of broadcasting, it is well known in almost every corner of the globe.

The music of the chimes has become a firmly established part of British heritage, among the best recognised sounds of Britain. Yet, how many of us, on hearing this famous tune would know its origin? Very few, I would suggest. In fact, the melody is based on a passage from Handel's *Messiah* and is an extension or, perhaps more correctly, an elaboration on a phrase in the aria 'I Know that my Redeemer Liveth'. Although synonymous with Westminster, the music had been in existence for more than sixty years before Big Ben struck his first hour, having been specially composed for the clock of Great St Mary's University Church in Cambridge, where it was introduced towards the end of the eighteenth century.

The church of St Mary the Great has a long and interesting history. The earliest record of a church on this site dates from the beginning of the thirteenth century, which shows that it was already well established as a place of worship. Little is known about the appearance of this early building for most of it was destroyed by fire in 1290. It was rebuilt, but only very slowly and over a period of many years; however, some parts of the original structure do remain. As the largest and most central church in Cambridge, it was natural that connections should be established with the growing university population. In particular, the church is proud of its ancient connection with Trinity College which has retained to this day the long-established right to appoint the vicar. In 1793, the original church clock, which had been installed in the latter part of the sixteenth century, was being replaced by a new clock built by Thwaites of London, and Joseph Jowett, Regius Professor of Civil Law was approached and asked to compose a chime. It may seem a little unlikely for a professor of law to be commissioned to write a piece of music, and in any event we cannot be sure whether the result is his, for traditionally it has been maintained, though almost entirely without any supporting evidence, that the melody was written either by Jowett in collaboration with Dr Randall, the Professor of Music, or, more probably entirely by Randall's brilliant young pupil and undergraduate William Crotch.

Crotch was a musical prodigy. Gifted with a natural ability from a very young age, as a child he toured extensively to give pianoforte recitals and is even said to have given a performance, when less than four years old, for King George III at Buckingham Palace. He studied at both Cambridge (where he played the organs of King's College, Trinity College and Great St Mary's) and Oxford where he became organist at Christ Church in 1790 and Professor of Music in 1797. Yet, despite all this, he was not a prolific composer, although he did write a number of sacred vocal anthems and some keyboard and chamber works. Interestingly, in later life he composed a large vocal ode called *The Bells* which requires an array of handbells to play the chimes of Oxford's various clocks. Although his name has long been forgotten, his works being seldom, if ever, performed nowadays, the music for the Cambridge quarters, as they were known originally, is seemingly immortal, having become familiar the world over as the Westminster chimes.

The fifth and sixth bars of Handel's aria 'I Know that my Redeemer Liveth', from *The Messiah*, used in the quarter-past chime.
(Peter Macdonald)

The chime was devised from the fifth bar of Handel's aria. These three notes, together with the first note of the following bar, comprise the first quarter or 'quarter past' chime, and it is from this, which is all that may be identified as Handel, that the other chimes were developed, each being different, as may be seen from the musical score.

The Westminster chimes. *(Peter Macdonald)*

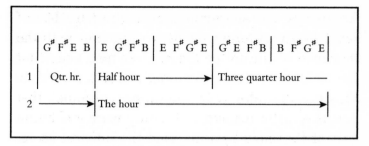

A diagram showing how the five phrases are combined to produce the four quarters. The chiming barrel revolves twice every hour.
(Peter Macdonald)

As has been noted already, the quarters at Westminster are chimed on the notes G sharp, F sharp, E and B and the hour is struck on E, one octave below the third quarter bell, so that the tune is set in the key of E major, as is the aria. Actually, the chiming barrel revolves twice during the course of each hour, and from the diagram it is interesting to follow how the five phrases are combined variously to produce the four quarters. The music is dignified and beautiful in its simplicity. When it was written Handel could have had no conception of how widely it would be played, for now there is hardly a country in the world where it is not heard.

For some sixty or more years the Cambridge quarters had been sounded only by the clock at Great St Mary's University Church and, in the normal course of events, that is how things might have stayed. But when Denison was an undergraduate at Cambridge, he heard these chimes

83

frequently and admired their elegance. He had remarked very often on how unfortunate it was that they could not be heard elsewhere and when he selected them for the Great Clock at Westminster, he took them out of obscurity, probably little realising that they were to become one of the most famous pieces of music in the world. At the time when the Westminster clock was designed there was no standard or regular chime – a clock could have its own, ranging from the simple 'ting tang' or 'ding dong' needing just two bells, to a vastly more complicated arrangement requiring perhaps eight or even ten bells, which produced such a noise that any melody was quite often lost. Barry's original plan had called for eight quarter bells but Denison purposely discarded this instruction and designed the mechanism to accept cams for just four bells. It seems that the notion of having eight bells had long been forgotten and this certainly turned out to be a blessing in disguise since it allowed Denison to select the chime of St Mary's. The Cambridge quarters are thought to be the oldest four bell clock chime in existence. There are others – Silchester and Dorking, for instance, but they do not have the dignity and majesty of Westminster, so Denison's choice has proved particularly fortunate.

Very little seems to have been written on the subject of clock chimes. However, an enlightening article 'The Song of the Hours', which collected chimes from around the British Isles, has been published in the *Horological Journal*: the organ of the British Horological Institute. From this it appears that while many will recognise just the Westminster sequence, several others are in existence. Norwich Cathedral, for instance, received a five bell chime which won a competition for the best set of chimes to be composed for the new clock in 1876. The award was won by the then Precentor of the cathedral, the aptly named Revd E.S. Medley. One of the most beautiful chimes is that composed for Holy Trinity Church, Guildford, in 1843 by George Wilkins, organist at the nearby Church of St Nicholas. It is sounded on eight bells and can be heard in several locations. The full chime prior to the hour is most impressive. Finally, mention can be made of the Whittington chime, composed in 1905 by Sir Charles Villiers Stanford for Bow church in London and based on the traditional six bell tune 'Turn again Whittington'. An eight bell variation is sometimes found on domestic clocks.

The visitor to Great St Mary's may hear the chimes sound over Cambridge just as they have done for more than two hundred years, though not so loudly. For in recent years the belfry has been boarded up to prevent 'nuisance' from the noise of the bells so that they can scarcely be heard, even in the Market Place below. This is most unfortunate, especially when one considers how little is ever done to reduce the nuisance caused by the continual roar of traffic and the increasing use of emergency sirens and intruder alarms. When the original clock was erected in 1577 it was silent and had an outside dial above the west door. Although in about 1590, when the belfry (which is in the tower above the west door) was completed, it had been proposed to introduce a chime to sound at every fourth hour. However, it was not until 1671 that one was set up to play two tunes on all eight bells at four, eight and twelve o'clock. In 1679 the dial was replaced by the one which is seen today. The chiming mechanism was taken out of use in 1722 when the old ring of eight bells was melted down and, by the addition of as much metal again, was cast into a new ring of ten by Richard Phelps of the Whitechapel Bell Foundry. Two new trebles were added in about 1770, so that by the time the Thwaites clock was installed in 1793 the ring had acquired its present number of twelve bells. The clock chimes the quarters on four of these bells, while the hour is struck on the tenor, that is the heaviest in the ring, which weighs 1 ton 7cwt 13lb, and sounds the note C sharp. These five bells are normally left in the 'down' position so that they can be struck by the external clock hammers. When they are required to be turned full circle for change ringing, the clock hammers are disengaged and the clock remains silent. In 1769, the tenor, or hour bell, as it was to become, fell from its frame while being rehung and was shattered. It was sent back to Whitechapel, where it was recast during the following year. The bell does not bear a name, but it does carry the following inscription: 'THIS BELL CAST IN THE YEAR OF OUR LORD 1770 ALDERMAN WEALES & JN HASELUM CH WARDENS PACK & CHAPMAN OF LONDON FECIT'. Messrs Pack & Chapman were by then the founders at Whitechapel. Some other members of the ring have also been recast, though none of those which chime the quarters. The Thwaites clock gave very nearly one hundred years' service to the church, but was replaced in 1892 by the present clock which was built by William Potts & Sons of Leeds. This clock incorporates many features which were introduced at Westminster, in particular the Grimthorpe double three-legged gravity escapement which is responsible for such good timekeeping.

Introducing the chimes to Westminster was not the first attempt to get the Cambridge quarters to London. When Edward Dent had completed his clock for the Royal Exchange in 1845, Denison had suggested those chimes for the quarters, and a variation of it does seem to have been introduced. Somehow the transcription was confused, with the result that the notes were played in the wrong order. Although this error was corrected some years afterwards, and the clock has chimed correctly ever since, it would seem that the Great Clock at Westminster was the first to use the chimes outside Cambridge. They soon became popular in London and have even acquired some lyrics. On an oak board prominently displayed on the wall of the clock room in the Palace of Westminster are the words which have been set to the music and which have become adopted as the 'Members' Prayer':

Words and Music of the Chimes

All through this hour
Lord be my Guide
That by Thy Power
No foot shall slide

Music from Handel's *Messiah*

The origin of the words is unknown, but they may have been inspired by a short hymn for four voices and organ, the music of which was based on the chimes, and which was published soon after the bells had been cast. Dedicated to Sir Charles Barry, the Palace's architect, it was composed by James Hine and entitled 'Lord in all our Counsels be our Guide'. The music of the chimes has also served as inspiration, even to the great composers. When Brahms's first symphony received its premiere in Cambridge – the very home of the chimes – the audience was surprised and much delighted to recognise the first notes of the Cambridge quarters in the rousing horn theme which forms part of the last movement. The notes of Big Ben are used to introduce the first movement of Vaughan Williams's *London Symphony* and are audible again before the end of the work. And, most significantly, a piece by the French composer Louis Vierne who lived during the early part of the twentieth century – the *Carillon de Westminster* from his Organ Suite No. 3 – is based entirely on the music of the chimes. They have also found their way into the world of light music; both Eric Coates's *Knightsbridge March* and Robert Farnon's *Westminster Waltz* include some very familiar phrases.

Since being adopted for Big Ben, the passages have become known as the Westminster chimes and, long established as the standard, have been copied on more public and domestic clocks than any other chime around the world. Yet, despite this, there appear to be few people, including musicians, who can sing, whistle or hum all four quarters without making a mistake. The hour should always be struck on the dominant, that is one octave below the third note of the first quarter, but this example has not been followed in every case, and the choice of another note for the hour can result in a less than pleasing arrangement.

The BBC began daily broadcasts of the chimes in 1924, and since then the chimes have been heard by millions around the globe. During the Second World War the chimes took on a particular significance, uniting listeners in the United Kingdom and overseas. Since it has become possible to reproduce the chimes digitally, the music has been used for electronic door bells and so on. Perhaps in fairness to the university city they should be known as the Cambridge quarters, but their use by the Great Clock at the Houses of Parliament has ensured that they will forever remain the Westminster chimes. By whichever name they are called, the chimes are as much a symbol of Britain as the clock tower itself.

6

Pennies on the Pendulum

The condition of accuracy which the Astronomer Royal had laid down for the Great Clock demanded that the first blow of each hour be struck to within a second of the time, then deemed an impossible level of accuracy, particularly for a large turret clock. In the end, after so many delays and uncertainties, it was due almost entirely to Dent's skill and expertise and to Denison's genius and determination that this apparently unattainable condition was satisfied and that such accuracy was not only achieved but has also been maintained from the very first tick in 1859. Of course, as with any machine, the performance of a pendulum clock depends not only upon its design but also on the level of workmanship and we may be sure that Dent's meticulous craftsmen applied the very highest standards of manufacture throughout. In the construction of the clock there are two areas where the greatest precision is critical: the escapement which allows the power of the weights to escape to the hands, and the pendulum which maintains a regular beat, thus allowing the clock to keep time.

In the mid-nineteenth century, when the clock was being designed, it was believed that no escapement then in existence was capable of meeting the required standard of accuracy. During the long period when the clock's movement was complete and being kept in Dent's workshop, Denison experimented with several types of escapement. First he tried various forms of the 'dead beat' variety. These worked well over a period of several months, but Denison was not satisfied, mainly because he knew that the clock's performance would be affected adversely as soon as the hands were exposed to the external pressures of wind and rain, so he set about developing an improved form of escapement.

The problem which Denison had to overcome was the same which had baffled horologists for ages: how to detach the pendulum from the going train, so that the stresses and strains from the elements exerting their forces against the hands could not be reflected back to affect the smooth running of the clock. The answer was the gravity escapement which lifts and locks two gravity arms instead of sending an impulse directly to the pendulum. After a great deal of experiment Denison designed a single three-legged gravity escapement. This was to be the breakthrough which had eluded horologists for so long, a true gravity escapement. Yet Airy, the Astronomer Royal, remained unconvinced and would not allow it to be fitted to the Westminster Clock, saying that he had proved mathematically that it was a failure. He did, however, agree to the escapement being tried out on a clock in the Greenwich Observatory where it proved to be a success. In the light of this, Airy appears to have revised his opinion, for he wrote to Denison: 'I have tried your escapement in the most malicious way, and shall endeavour to get it into Westminster'. Although this must have come as a welcome endorsement, it was regarded very much as a formality because Denison had, by now, virtually taken sole charge of the project.

This initial success seems to have spurred Denison on for he immediately set about designing an improvement and came up with the four-legged gravity escapement. This did offer some advance on the original, but still he believed that there was room for improvement and carried on working towards the perfect escapement. Eventually, he hit upon it – the double three-legged gravity escapement, which was the horologist's dream come true. It has the advantage over its predecessors of reducing the pressure on the gravity arms still further to the absolute minimum required – so that the pendulum is kept swinging by the very smallest of forces.

Interestingly, although the double three-legged gravity escapement was designed specifically for Big Ben, it was fitted in the first instance to a clock situated a third of the way around the world. As the mechanism of the Great Clock was still on

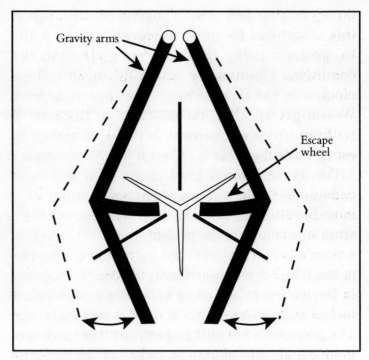

A Grimthorpe double three-legged gravity escapement. Each arm is opened and closed alternately by the swing of the pendulum, releasing and locking the wheel. *(Peter Macdonald)*

test in Dent's workshop, awaiting the completion of the clock tower, the opportunity was taken to try out the new escapement under far more severe conditions than were ever likely to be encountered at Westminster. Dent had recently completed a clock for the cathedral at Fredericton in New Brunswick, Canada, where winter temperatures may fall to 30 or 40 degrees below freezing and where very heavy snowfalls are to be expected.

So it was decided to test the new escapement on this clock. The escapement was fitted and found to perform very well under such extreme conditions of snow, ice and wind. Although the clock was not as large or as heavy as the one at Westminster, the experiment demonstrated without any doubt the superiority of the new escapement.

The double three-legged gravity escapement is considered to be the ultimate and is one of the most beautifully thought out and remarkable, yet simple, mechanisms ever invented. A working example is on display in the horological collection at the Old Royal Observatory at Greenwich and it is fascinating to watch as each arm is alternately locked and unlocked while the pendulum swings. The success of this escapement became apparent immediately, and a notable aspect of its invention is that although the gravity escapement was considered to represent the greatest advance in turret clock design for many centuries, no attempt appears to have been made to patent it. In fact Dent, in his book *Clock and Watch Work*, writes: 'as it is not patented, it may be made by anybody'. Considering that the escapement had completely solved such a long-standing horological problem any patent rights would undoubtedly have been of great financial value, yet Denison never showed any desire to make money out of his long years of tireless work spent perfecting the Westminster Clock. For Denison the aim was purely the advancement of horology, and he seems to have made every effort to persuade as many clock-makers as possible to adopt the new escapement, for he became very annoyed with those who refused to do so. The escapement is the major feature of the clock and the main reason for its excellent timekeeping. It was soon adopted as the standard and remains unaltered to this day, having since been incorporated in most turret clocks around the world. It is a tribute to its inventor that the escapements on so many clocks by other makers, including the clock at St Paul's Cathedral, are marked 'Grimthorpe's double three-legged escapement'. In many ways this is a misnomer, since at the time of its invention Denison was still a commoner. Perhaps it should be called, more correctly, the Denison escapement.

The pendulum inside the Great Clock is 13ft long and swings every two seconds, which makes for a very slow and imposing beat. It is suspended from the pendulum cock (suspension bracket), which is a massive cast iron structure set into the wall of the clock room, and is thus completely free of interference from any vibration which might be caused by the mechanism or the bells. The pendulum is suspended from the cock by the pendulum spring, a piece of very thin spring steel which allows the pendulum to swing freely, while coming into contact only with the escapement. In order that the required level of accuracy may be achieved, it is essential that the pendulum be

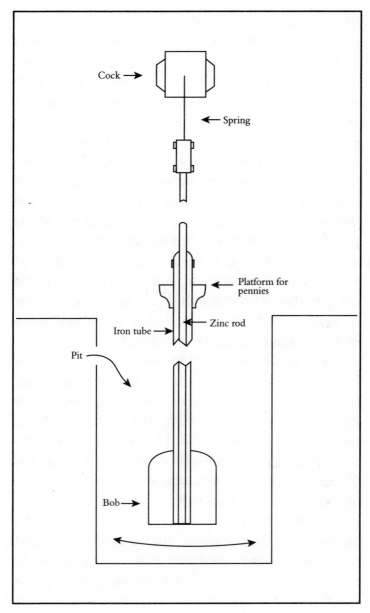

The Pendulum. *(Peter Macdonald)*

protected from as many external influences as possible. Any change in the ambient temperature or barometric pressure could affect the clock's performance very seriously. To keep the pendulum insulated as far as practicable from the effects of air currents, the greater part of its length is encased within the pendulum pit, a cast iron box about 10ft deep which has been sunk into the floor of the clock room. To compensate for changes in temperature, and in an effort to allow the length of the pendulum to remain constant, Denison had the pendulum comprise a rod of zinc set within an iron tube so that any expansion or contraction in one of the metals should counter a similar effect on the other. Through a flash of ingenuity, the tube is slotted so that any variation in temperature reaches each component simultaneously.

The original specification required the time kept by the Great Clock at Westminster to be telegraphed to Greenwich so that the clock's performance could be compared with the exact time as maintained by the Royal Observatory. For this purpose, electric contacts were provided behind the dial within the mechanism in the clock room and in 1863 a line was installed between Westminster and Greenwich to allow for the transmission of the signal. The Westminster clock received a signal from the observatory once on every hour, thus allowing the operator in the clock room to note and compensate for any error. The clock also reported its own state by transmitting a signal twice a day, at noon and midnight, to Greenwich where it was compared with the correct time as measured by the observatory. A daily record of the clock's performance was completed at the observatory where it was soon found that the level of accuracy was well within the limits which had been prescribed originally. In the Astronomer Royal's report for that first year Airy noted that 'the rate of this clock may be considered certain to much less than one second per week'.

The clock has always been allowed to run independently and has never been corrected by any signal received from the observatory, so despite the precautions which have been mentioned already, if it were left to its own devices, it would drift very gradually and present an ever increasing error, so a very simple method was contrived to allow for the final adjustment to be made by hand. It was known that if the pendulum's centre of gravity could be raised it would swing more quickly and the clock would gain time, while if its centre of gravity could be lowered it would swing more slowly and the clock would lose time. Not far from the top of the pendulum there is a tray on which have been placed a number of imperial pennies and halfpennies. The addition of a penny will cause the clock to gain 0.4 of a second in a period of twenty-four hours, assuming that there is no change in the barometric conditions. Removing a penny causes the clock to lose a similar amount.

By using halfpennies the effect is halved. This system has proved to be very effective throughout the life of the clock and presently the 'pendulum fund' consists of several pennies and halfpennies. Unfortunately, it is no longer possible to compare the clock's rate with a signal from the observatory because the special telegraph line was destroyed by the Luftwaffe during the Second World War. It was not considered worth the expense of renewing it, as after seventy-five years of daily comparison it was felt that the clock's accuracy had been more than amply demonstrated. In any event, the Royal Observatory moved to Herstmonceux Castle near Hailsham in Sussex during the 1950s, and eventually to Cambridge until its closure in 1998. The final report, issued from the observatory in 1939, showed the error to have been greater than one second on sixteen days during the previous year, but on more than 180 days (about six months) the error was less than half a second. An excellent record, and one which is still easily maintained.

For obvious reasons, due to its singular nature, the responsibility for maintaining the Great Clock has always been entrusted to a specialist clock-maker. For more than the first hundred years of its life this work was carried out by the clock's builder, Messrs E. Dent & Company. Their contract included winding, regulating and adjusting for accuracy, and a programme of regular inspection and routine maintenance. They also undertook to provide a twenty-four hour call-out service so that a representative would be available to attend at any time, day or night, should there be a failure of the mechanism. However, by the beginning of the 1970s Dent & Company were finding it increasingly difficult to recruit experienced clockworkers to replace those who were approaching retirement, and they asked to be allowed to terminate their contract. This was put out to tender and in 1971 it was awarded to Messrs Thwaites & Reed, a very long-established company with a fine reputation for turret clocks. It will be remembered that although they had been refused the opportunity to tender for the construction of the Great Clock, it was to be Thwaites & Reed who would rebuild it after the catastrophe in 1976. While the shortage of skilled clockworkers was already serious over thirty years ago, with the evolution of quartz movements and radio controlled devices the situation is far worse today. A further change took place in 2002, since when the maintenance of the clock has been undertaken directly by the Parliamentary Works Directorate.

Currently the clock is wound and checked for accuracy three times a week, normally on Monday, Wednesday and Friday. Although the going train, which drives the hands and controls the operation of both the chiming and the striking trains, has the capacity to run for about ten days, it is still wound at each inspection to allow for sickness or any other unforseen circumstance. It takes over an hour to wind, by hand, the length of cable which has been used over the previous two or three days. The chiming and striking trains are much heavier. For more than fifty years these too were wound by hand but this was found to be very laborious, taking two men several hours to complete. In 1912 Dent's installed an electric winder and since then these two larger trains have been wound by this method, which is entirely satisfactory. As a time signal is no longer received directly from the Royal Observatory, the operator checks the clock's performance against the telephone speaking clock by using a stopwatch and records in the log any error, together with the barometric pressure. Coins can then be added to or removed from the pendulum if required. It is interesting that although decimal currency has been in use for more than thirty years, imperial coins have been retained for placing on the pendulum as their effect is well known, having been in continual use for more than a hundred years. However, after the serious mechanical failure in 1976 which left the chimes silent for many months, to mark the reconstruction of the chiming mechanism in time for the Queen's visit to the Palace of Westminster on the occasion of her Silver Jubilee in the following year, a number of pennies were replaced by a specially minted crown.

Although the Definition of Time Act had become law in 1880 making Greenwich Mean Time the legal standard for the whole of the United Kingdom, the idea of advancing clocks by one hour during the summer months was not considered until the early years of the twentieth century. It was the brainchild of William Willett, a businessman. Willett, who had established a reputation as the builder of fine houses, argued that the early hours of daylight on summer mornings were wasted as most of the population were still asleep and did not rise until after it had been light for some time. He maintained that rising early would benefit the economy by reducing dependence on artificial light and would result in considerable savings in energy consumption, and he also reasoned that it would have a beneficial effect on the nation's health. He proposed that clocks be put forward in the spring by one hour, and put back again in the autumn. 'If people can adjust their watches at sea, day by day, without discomfort,' he said, 'why not on land twice a year?' This proposal met with considerable opposition, even ridicule, and Willett faced an uphill struggle lasting some years before he was taken seriously. As early as 1907 he circulated a pamphlet outlining his proposals to Members of Parliament and other parties, and meetings were held and addressed by well-known speakers illustrating the advantages of the scheme.

In 1909 the Daylight Saving Bill was drafted, but in spite of a growing measure of support it was not until 1916 that the Daylight Saving Act was passed, and then only as a wartime measure, advancing clocks by one hour during the period of operation. This was a brilliant idea but had it not been for the need to maintain stringent economy brought about by the outbreak of the First World War, it may not have been accepted so readily. During that first year of operation clocks were advanced only for the period from 21 May until 1 October. Summer Time has been adopted in every year since, the position being stabilised by the Summer Time Act of 1925. This provided that clocks be put forward on the day after the third Saturday in April (or, if that is Easter Day, then one week earlier), and put back on the day after the first Saturday in October. Since then the period of operation has been gradually increased through an Order in Council – currently summer time is in force from the end of March until the end of October, more than half the year. The measure proved to be so effective that in some years during the Second World War, and again in 1947, when the need for economy was at its greatest, Double Summer Time – two hours in advance of Greenwich Mean Time – became the legal standard.

Between 1968 and 1971 an experiment was carried out whereby 'summer time' remained in force throughout the year. One hour ahead of GMT, this was known as British Standard Time, and recently there have been proposals to adopt the system permanently, with a further adjustment for the summer, mainly to bring the United Kingdom into line with continental Europe. However, opposition is strong, especially in the north and west where, in the depths of winter, sunrise would not occur until very late. Although the period during which summer time is in operation was originally decided by Parliament, for some years the dates have been set by the European Union. This situation became apparent during the autumn of 1995 when British Summer Time was due to end on the last Sunday in October, but the EU ruled that Britain should revert to Greenwich Mean Time one week earlier and the government complied. Willett died in 1915, so he did not live to see his scheme come to fruition. Since then the practice of advancing clocks during the summer months has been adopted in many parts of the world. So that William Willett should not be forgotten, in 1927 a sundial showing summer time was erected in his home town of Petts Wood in Kent.

As far as the Great Clock is concerned the change to or from British Summer Time offers the advantage of allowing the movement to be stopped for a few hours twice a year in order that some inspection and routine maintenance work can be carried out. Obviously, more time is available in the autumn when the clocks are put back. The usual procedure is for the clock to chime 9.45 on the evening of the changeover; then the lights behind the dials are switched off, the pendulum is disengaged, the clock is stopped and the chiming and striking mechanisms are also disconnected. The hands, now practically invisible, are set to midnight in order not to cause confusion to anyone who is able to see them, even against the darkened dial. The maintenance work is scheduled to be completed by midnight (at the new time), when the pendulum is engaged and the clock is started, but still in darkness and still silent as the new time would not yet be legal. For many years the new time became law at 2 a.m. GMT, but nowadays the change is made at 1 a.m. At about ten minutes before the new time comes into operation, 2 a.m. in the spring or 1 a.m. in the autumn, the chiming and striking mechanisms are re-engaged, then at one minute to the hour the dial lights are switched on and the clock strikes the hour. As Big Ben normally broadcasts the time at midnight on Radio 4, on these occasions when the bells are not available, the Great Clock is replaced by the Greenwich Time Signal.

7

On the Air

On New Year's Eve 1923 the British Broadcasting Company, as it was known initially, arranged a special surprise for listeners. A few days earlier a microphone had been set up on the roof of a nearby building, No. 1 Bridge Street, just opposite the Houses of Parliament. As the time approached midnight the chimes of the Great Clock ringing out the old year were followed on the hour by the twelve deep strokes of Big Ben ringing in the new, and broadcast, by means of a temporary line running to the control room at Savoy Hill, to listeners tuned to 2LO, the BBC's first radio transmitter, then barely a year old. This was Big Ben's first appearance 'on the air' and although it was available to a very limited audience, it did mark the beginning of what has turned out to be one of the very longest careers in the history of broadcasting. However, it was not the first attempt to provide a radio time signal.

The BBC had commenced broadcasting in November 1922 from premises in the Strand, moving the following February to No. 2 Savoy Hill, and it is believed that in these early days an announcer would sometimes play the Westminster chimes on a piano in the studio in an effort to approximate the time. In the spring of 1923 the BBC invited Frank Hope-Jones, Chairman of the Wireless Society of London and a great pioneer and authority on electric clocks, to announce the putting forward of the clocks at the changeover to summer time. Hope-Jones was also known to have been an enthusiastic supporter of William Willett's daylight saving proposals and on the evening of 21 April, the day before the introduction of BST, he broadcast a short talk on timekeeping which he concluded by giving a countdown, from his own pocket watch, of the last five seconds before 10 p.m. This was the first BBC time signal, and it appears to have inspired Hope-Jones to suggest the transmission of a signal giving Greenwich Mean Time directly from the observatory. This proposal was eagerly accepted by the BBC and Hope-Jones was appointed as the 'time consultant' with responsibility for putting the scheme into effect.

Meanwhile, Big Ben's broadcast on New Year's Eve had proved to be very popular, with the BBC receiving scores of letters of congratulation from listeners keen to know if the chimes were to be heard on a regular basis. Hence it was not long before the Great Clock was appointed to their permanent staff. However, the Greenwich Time Signal, consisting of the now familiar 'six pips', was the first to be heard regularly. It was introduced on 5 February 1924 via a direct line from the Royal

Observatory at Greenwich and was provided initially by one of Dent's regulators, with another on standby in case of failure. Although the clock had been built half a century earlier in 1874, it was still extremely accurate and remained in service, giving the time signal over the air, until 1949. It now forms part of the horological collection on view in the Old Royal Observatory at Greenwich, where it continues to give the time signal every fifteen minutes. The signal consists of six pips, each created by the oscillation of a valve in the control room, and each separated from the next by an interval of one second. The signal begins at five seconds before the minute, so that it is the last pip which denotes the time. Hope-Jones was once asked why there are six pips in the signal. He is said to have replied: 'Six is one more than five.' This is not a very enlightening answer by any standard, but it must be said that the number of pips does sound just about right.

Although Big Ben's New Year appearance had proved to be a great success with listeners, this initial broadcast had demonstrated that a microphone placed outside the clock tower would pick up too much interference, mainly from traffic noise, to allow for regular broadcasting of an acceptable quality. So when, during the early days of 1924, the BBC planned the introduction of daily transmissions, their engineers experimented by fixing a microphone in the belfry. After carrying out various tests, it was found that the best result was obtained by placing the microphone in a

football bladder which had been located immediately above the gantries from where the bells are
suspended. This rather unusual method made for
reception of a reasonable quality and it remained
in use for some years until the development of
more sophisticated microphones. Daily broadcasting of the Great Clock was inaugurated on
17 February 1924, and, with just a few interruptions, it has continued ever since. In these very
early days the clock gave the time on all
wavelengths at 7 p.m. on weekdays and at 3 p.m.
on Sundays with additional broadcasts for the
London area at the end of the evening on
weekdays, at 8.30 p.m. on Sundays and at 1 p.m.
on Tuesdays, Thursdays and Fridays. Unlike the
Greenwich Time Signal, it is the first stroke of Big
Ben which gives the hour, while the first note of
each chime denotes the quarter.

In 1932 the BBC moved to Broadcasting House
in Langham Place, which has remained its head-
quarters ever since, and with the inauguration in
December that year of the Empire Broadcasting
Service – the forerunner of today's World Service –
it became possible for listeners around the globe to
hear the bells. On Christmas Day, with the new
service just six days old, the BBC undertook an
amazing link-up. The programme began with Big
Ben striking 2 p.m., and for one short hour that
afternoon messages of peace and goodwill were
sent from London and relayed from station to
station, right around the world. Although listeners

in Britain were suffering a cold winter's day, those in South Africa were sweltering in a glorious summer afternoon and, in Australia, where it was already past midnight, the broadcasters recounted the intense heat of the previous day. In India it was 8 p.m., while in parts of Canada a frosty Christmas dawn was breaking, and in New Zealand and Fiji it was already 2 or 3 a.m. on Boxing Day morning. The link passed from one continent to another with each country making a contribution. Time, temperatures and cultures might vary but the message was universal – so many peoples united through the radio and under the symbol of Big Ben, familiar, majestic and yet friendly. The programme was followed at 3 p.m. by the Westminster chimes, and as the last stroke of Big Ben died away, King George V delivered the first Christmas message, spoken from his fireside at Sandringham. His Majesty was obviously very enthusiastic about the possibilities offered by the developments in wireless telegraphy, for in a part of his broadcast he said:

Through one of the marvels of modern science I am enabled this Christmas Day to speak to all my people throughout the Empire. I take it as a good omen that the wireless should have reached its present perfection at a time when the Empire has been linked in closer union, for it affords us immense opportunities to make that union closer still . . . I speak now from my own home and from my heart to you all, to men and women so cut off by the snows and the deserts, or the seas, that only the voices out of the air can reach them . . . It may be that our future will lay upon us more than one stern task. Our past will have taught us how to meet it unshaken.

There seems to have been some hint of foreboding in the King's words, for he refers to 'one stern task' which might lie ahead; the Second World War was, by then, less than seven years away.

From that time the sound of the bells has always introduced the Christmas message, but although for many years it has been the custom to record the broadcast some weeks beforehand, the chimes which precede it on Christmas afternoon are always live, something of which the BBC is justifiably proud.

In 1934, after the clock had ticked up seventy-five years of continuous timekeeping over London, including ten years of broadcasting on the radio, it was found necessary to undertake a major overhaul, mainly on the bells, and for two months during the late spring and early summer Great Tom, the clock of St Paul's Cathedral, announced the time over the airwaves. Great Tom appeared to be very welcome on the radio and proved an admirable deputy, but listeners were pleased to be reunited with Big Ben on his return.

By the outbreak of the Second World War in September 1939, the Great Clock at Westminster had already become established as the national timepiece, and it was during those six long dark years of conflict that Big Ben would take on a special significance, as will be seen in the next chapter. In particular, during the early part of the war it was decided to replace the Greenwich Time Signal with the full 9 p.m. strike immediately before the nightly news bulletin on the Home Service. This became known as the 'Big Ben Minute' and its purpose was to unite listeners in a moment of quiet thought and reflection. This arrangement continued not only until the end of the war but also for many years afterwards, and the broadcasting of the bells did much to boost morale, both at home and overseas.

On New Year's Eve 1949, after a quarter of a century of broadcasting, Big Ben entered the world of television. Of course, the service offered in that medium by the BBC was still in its infancy and few households were equipped with a receiver, but cameras had been set up on the roof of St Thomas's Hospital just across the Thames from the Houses of Parliament and viewers were able to see as well as hear the Great Clock striking in the new year, as they have been able to do every year since. In fact, New Year's Eve without Big Ben would come to seem unthinkable.

Inevitably, the years of war took their toll on the clock – the tower had been damaged during the Blitz – and in 1956 it was decided to erect scaffolding around the clock tower to facilitate the repair of the masonry and ironwork. The opportunity was also taken to do some more work on the bells and, once again, Great Tom deputised on the radio. The work was much more extensive than on the previous occasion, and this time the cathedral clock was on the air for almost six months from early July until late December, Big Ben being brought back into service just in time for Christmas and the new year.

By 1960 times were changing and the Home Service was losing many listeners to the more recently introduced television service. This prompted the BBC to implement a number of revisions to their evening radio schedules, one of which was to affect the broadcasting of Big Ben. First, it was decided not to continue with the entire nine o'clock strike on the Home Service. The final Big Ben Minute was broadcast on 17 September 1960 – thereafter the main evening news was moved to ten o'clock and the strokes were faded out. Big Ben survived for almost another ten years in the ten o'clock spot, the last appearance being made on 3 April 1970, after which the clock was replaced by the 'six pips'. However, for a few years towards the end of the 1980s the evening news and current affairs pro- gramme *The World Tonight* on Radio 4, as the Home Service had become, was broadcast at 10.30 p.m. and was introduced by the chimes of Big Ben. Since 1 January 1972 the Greenwich Time Signal has been modified, the sixth pip being lengthened for identification. It is the start of this pip which gives the time.

The chimes suffered their longest absence from the airwaves after the clock underwent a major mechanical failure in August 1976. Metal fatigue destroyed much of the chiming mechanism and although the clock was able to strike the hours, Great Tom was brought in once more, particularly for the World Service where the quarters were broadcast many times a day. This was the worst disaster to take place since the clock had been built; with so much of the mechanism destroyed and needing to be rebuilt the chimes could not be sounded for nine months until May 1977. During this period both Tom and Ben were employed to broadcast the time, Great Tom being heard mainly on Radio 3 and Big Ben only striking the hours on Radio 4.

When the Great Clock was inspected during the change to GMT in October 1987, cracks were discovered in part of the striking mechanism. As a precaution striking was discontinued, but fortunately the clock carried on chiming, and it was only necessary to take the great bell out of service for a week. During this time, on the radio, at the hour the chimes were either broadcast without the strike or replaced entirely by the Greenwich Time Signal.

Since its inception in 1924, the 'six pips' time signal had been generated by the Royal Observatory. In 1990, the observatory moved from Herstmonceux to Cambridge, and it was decided to cease production of the by now world famous time signal. Since 5 February 1990 the 'pips' have been generated by the BBC from three pairs of computer clocks and a rubidium oscillator situated in the bowels of Broadcasting House. Listeners have never noticed any difference because the signal continues to be broadcast at the regular times and sounds exactly the same as before.

In March 1990 signs of metal fatigue were found to be developing in Big Ben's striking hammer arm and *The Times* reported that the hour bell would be silent 'for three months'. In fact, the replacement of the hammer arm took much longer than anticipated and although the Great Clock continued chiming, it was unable to strike the hours until the end of August. On this occasion no attempt appears to have been made to broadcast Great Tom, and although Big Ben was retained for broadcasting at the quarters, any hourly appearance on the air was replaced by the Greenwich Time Signal. The powers that be in Broadcasting House considered that the new hammer arm had altered the tone of Big Ben rendering it 'awful', and refused to broadcast it, except, of course on Remembrance Day. Eventually they relented and the clock returned to the airwaves during December, just in time for Christmas and the new year.

There can be no doubt that the advent of broadcasting has made Big Ben a radio star. Late in his life, when the Great Clock had overcome its initial troubles and was becoming established as the foremost timekeeper in the land, Lord Grimthorpe had expressed his wish that there could be some way of sending a time signal to every town and village; how appropriate that it should be the Westminster Clock, which he designed and for whose completion he had campaigned so tirelessly, that would fulfil his wish. Although Big Ben broadcasts the time on the radio every day of the year, the 'six pips' Greenwich Time Signal is used far more frequently, being transmitted on most of the BBC national radio networks and heard many times a week. Regrettably, Big Ben's regular broadcasting schedule has declined over the years. It was probably at its height during and for some time after the Second World War, when the bells gave the time on both the Home Service and the Light Programme. Throughout this period the chimes were heard both at the beginning and the end of daily broadcasting which, quite apart from indicating the time, maintained an additional role for the clock in identifying the BBC. Since the introduction of 24-hour broadcasting, this distinction would be more difficult to achieve. It may seem hard to believe today, but in the very early days of Radio 1 during the late 1960s, the chimes of Big Ben were broadcast every morning at 5.30, immediately after the now legendary *Theme One*, the anthem specially composed and played by George Martin and his orchestra. Today, the clock is heard regularly fifteen times a week on Radio 4: every evening at 6 p.m. and at midnight and additionally on Sunday evenings at

10 p.m. The Greenwich Time Signal is broadcast at most hours on Radio 4 and to a much lesser extent on other networks. Fortunately, listeners in many parts of the world may hear the chimes every day on the overseas broadcasts of the BBC World Service, although regrettably not in the United Kingdom, as regular broadcasting of the clock on the English language service was discontinued in about 1999. Hopefully, as the 150th anniversary of Big Ben approaches, the BBC will reconsider the matter and reinstate the clock on this wavelength.

But it is the special broadcasts which are probably the most memorable. As the nation's bell, Big Ben is unique in being identified with both joyful and solemn occasions, the music of the chimes being associated equally with celebration and reflection. Apart from broadcasting the time, the Great Clock undertakes a number of 'official duties' which are broadcast throughout the land. Every year, during the ceremony at the Cenotaph in Whitehall on Remembrance Day the chimes prepare the British people for the two minutes' silence at 11 a.m. during which the nation remembers those who gave their lives in the service of their country, not only during the two world wars but also in many other conflicts. Between the firing of the guns, which signal both the beginning and the end of the silence, the eleven strokes of Big Ben are the only sounds permitted. Since the inception of broadcasting, Big Ben has failed to lead the nation's remembrance on just one occasion, in 1956, when the clock was nearing the end of its major overhaul and the work just fell short of completion in time for Remembrance Day. In 1976, although Big Ben sounded the eleven strokes as usual, the preceding chimes remained silent as their mechanism had been almost completely destroyed by metal fatigue during the previous August and was still awaiting repair. During the silence the bells are broadcast on all five BBC national radio stations and all BBC national television channels. In recent years it has become the practice to observe the silence on 11 November, whether or not it falls on a Sunday, and for this reason in most years there are now two remembrance days, and Big Ben is broadcast on both. On New Year's Eve the sound of the bells is broadcast at midnight on both BBC radio and television. These two occasions, Remembrance Day and New Year's Eve, illustrate to the greatest effect how the clock, as the symbol of Britain, is associated with both the solemnity of remembrance and hope for the new year. Occasionally Big Ben is called upon to replace the Greenwich Time Signal on the radio when the following news bulletin features an item of sufficient magnitude such as a ministerial resignation.

Although the Greenwich Time Signal was given on BBC television during its very early years, Big Ben has never been used purely as a time signal for viewers – the sound of the bells has been broadcast solely on special occasions. However, the clock is often seen and heard during news bulletins and current affairs programmes which feature reports from Westminster. The bells have become synonymous not only with ceremony and pageantry but also with thanksgiving and rejoicing. Somehow, replacing them with the 'six pips' of the Greenwich Time Signal just wouldn't seem the same.

When the Great Clock was started in 1859, the concept of wireless telegraphy sill lay over forty years in the future, yet it is only by that means that the clock has been heard in almost every home and the sound of the bells has been made instantly recognisable to people the world over. That surprise broadcast on New Year's Eve 1923 was to take the Great Clock into a new era – one which could never have been envisioned at the time of the clock's conception. Big Ben has been on the air almost since the beginning of radio and has now achieved over eighty years of regular broadcasting, in the process becoming a radio superstar, loved by millions around the globe.

8

Big Ben during Wartime

This morning the British ambassador in Berlin handed the German government a final note stating that unless we heard from them by eleven o'clock that they were prepared at once to withdraw their troops from Poland a state of war would exist between us. I have to tell you now that no such undertaking has been received, and that consequently this country is at war with Germany.

These famous words, broadcast to the nation as they were spoken by the Prime Minister, Neville Chamberlain, from the Cabinet Room at 10 Downing Street at 11.15 on the morning of Sunday 3 September 1939 marked the outbreak of the Second World War and the beginning of the darkest period in Britain's history.

Following the completion of the Great Clock in 1859, Britain had enjoyed many decades of peace and stability. Of course, its forces had been involved in the Boer War in South Africa between 1899 and 1902, but the action was so far away and communications so difficult that hardly any effects were felt at home. So it was not until the outbreak of the First World War in 1914 that the prospect of aerial attack, and in particular the likelihood of Zeppelin raids over London, had to be considered. The Zeppelins were very quiet, low-flying airships, and when raids were expected in 1916 it was feared that the sound of the clock bells might disclose the whereabouts of Parliament to the enemy. Accordingly, it was decided that the clock should not be heard while this threat remained, and so the striking and chiming mechanisms were disengaged and the bells remained silent until the end of the war – their longest silence in the clock's history. So there was much rejoicing in London when the bells were restored at 11 a.m. on 11 November 1918 when they rang out to mark the signing of the Armistice and the end of hostilities. As Big Ben announced the victorious end of the First World War the people of London filled the streets in their thousands to hear the joyful news that the horrors of the conflict were at an end. At the sound of the bells the war-straitened, regulated streets had erupted into a triumphant pandemonium of rejoicing.

By the outbreak of the Second World War in 1939 the Great Clock at Westminster was already firmly established as the national timepiece, and because aeroplanes were now flying at much higher altitudes it was not considered necessary to silence the clock bells. Moreover, it was thought that the music of the chimes would be reassuring, especially at a time when the ringing of church bells was prohibited – they were to be sounded only as a warning in the event of an invasion. However, in keeping with the blackout regulations, the lights behind the clock dials and the Ayrton Light were extinguished on 1 September, just prior to the outbreak of war. During the following year, Big Ben was to be called to a still higher purpose than could ever have been imagined when the lights had been switched off, and the Great Clock would be destined to play a significant part in the survival of the free peoples of the world.

From the beginning of the war the Greenwich Time Signal had been broadcast every day just before the main evening news at 9 p.m. on the Home Service. During the early part of 1940 a body consisting of many senior churchmen, Members of Parliament and other prominent people approached the BBC, suggesting that they discontinue the Greenwich Time Signal in favour of Big Ben. (Incidentally, the clock felt the effects of the war when the special telegraph line, which had been laid between Westminster and Greenwich in 1863 for the purpose of relaying the clock's performance to the observatory, was destroyed by the Luftwaffe during a raid in 1940.) Meanwhile, the BBC were very sympathetic to this request and agreed to replace the six pips with Big Ben's 9 p.m. strike. On Remembrance Day, Sunday 10 November 1940, at a time when Britain stood virtually alone against Hitler's Germany, the Great

Clock took over the 9 p.m. spot and the 'Big Ben Minute' was inaugurated. This was a solemn moment – people were urged to keep silent wherever they were for one minute during the sounding of the chimes and the nine strokes, and to think of the men and women in the armed forces, many of whom were never to return, and of the struggle for a just and free world. The objects of this 'dedicated minute', as it was known, were officially given as: 'To provide an opportunity for people of goodwill at home and overseas to unite in dedicating themselves for one minute each evening at nine o'clock, to God's service in prayer and silence.' A pamphlet entitled *The Big Ben Silent Minute Observance* was issued, containing short passages from the scriptures and other words of inspiration.

For many around the world, 9 p.m. was unsuitable, due to the difference in time, and the BBC received several requests from listeners in distant parts for the chimes to be broadcast at more practical hours. This was agreed and Big Ben was heard many times a day on overseas programmes, enabling those around the world to share in the comradeship of the bells. In New Zealand, where the time difference from London is about half a day, a recording of the 9 p.m. strike was played every evening on all radio stations. Like the music of Glenn Miller and the swing bands which has come to be regarded as the soundtrack for the Second World War, the sound of the bells did much to raise morale and lift the spirits of many whose lives had been shattered during those dark years; it was the American servicemen stationed in Britain who are said to have christened the chimes the 'signature tune of the British Empire', more symbolic of London even than Bow Bells. The Big Ben Minute became somewhat of an institution, serving as a focal point for reflection and symbolising the nation's unity and determination. It was not forgotten at the end of the war and continued for a further fifteen years.

During the war the Houses of Parliament were bombed on at least a dozen occasions, three of which resulted in significant damage. In September 1940 a high explosive bomb landed in Old Palace Yard, severely damaging the southern wall of St Stephen's Porch and causing minor damage to the statue of Richard the Lionheart, which appeared to have been lifted out of its pedestal. Just three months later, in December, another high explosive bomb fell nearby, this time demolishing the southern and eastern sides of the cloisters and causing serious damage to the other two sides. But on the night of 10/11 May 1941, at the height of the Blitz, the Palace of Westminster took a direct hit and the debating chamber of the Commons was totally destroyed. Luftwaffe records, discovered after the end of the war, revealed that this was not a deliberate or planned attack on the Houses of Parliament, but nevertheless, at least twelve separate incidents were recorded on this night in various parts of the building and three people are known to have been killed as a result. The Commons chamber was engulfed by fire which spread to the Members' Lobby, causing the ceiling to collapse. The roof of the centuries old Westminster Hall was also set on fire, while the House of Lords was struck by a bomb which passed through the floor of the chamber without exploding or causing any injury.

On the same night the clock tower was struck at the eaves of the metal roof, probably by a small bomb or an anti-aircraft shell. Some of the ornamental ironwork was destroyed and much of the stonework was damaged. The glass in the south dial was also completely shattered, although mercifully the clock and the bells remained unscathed. This was truly the worst night that Londoners had ever known and flames from the burning debris below reached as high as the clock tower itself. And yet, despite all this, Big Ben kept going with his usual accuracy, the clock's error that night being recorded as just less than a second and a half away from Double Summer Time, and continued to broadcast the time. If ever proof was needed that Big Ben is always broadcast live, this was it, because the sounds of the raid were picked up by the microphones in the belfry and carried to distant parts with the music of the bells. Many must have prayed that the Great Clock would be spared from destruction and must have been relieved to hear the bells again during the following days and weeks.

After the destruction of the Commons chamber, alternative accommodation was provided for both Houses of Parliament, initially in Church House for some short periods in May and June 1941, and again during the flying bomb attacks between June and August 1944. The Lords sat in the Hall of Convocation while the Commons used the Hoare Memorial Hall, where a tablet records their occupation. Eventually, and for the much greater part of the period from 1941 until the building of their new chamber had been completed, the Commons sat in the House of Lords, while the Lords made use of the Robing Room. In December 1943 a Select Committee chaired by Earl Winterton was appointed 'to consider and report upon plans for the rebuilding of the House of Commons and upon such alterations as may be considered desirable while preserving all its essential features'. However, it was not until after the war that the work of building the new chamber began. The Committee appointed Sir Giles Gilbert Scott as architect and Dr Oscar Faber as engineer, and both took great care to ensure that the reconstruction would blend in with the original façade. After their scheme had been approved by the Royal Fine Arts Commission and recommended by the Committee, it was agreed by Parliament in January 1945. Clearance of the site began in May of that year and the foundation stone was laid by the Speaker of the House, Colonel D. Clifton Brown, on 26 May 1948. The Commons met in their new chamber, which

retains the Gothic elegance of Barry's masterpiece,
for the first time on 26 October 1950. Also present
in the gallery on that special occasion were the
speakers or presiding officers from the legislatures of
twenty-eight Common-wealth countries. Since
television cameras have been allowed into the House
of Commons, this debating chamber has become
familiar to viewers throughout Britain and further
afield with the BBC Parliament channel. The Lords
returned to their own chamber just over six months
later, in May 1951.

Amazingly, despite coming within a whisker of
being destroyed on that terrible night in May 1941,
Big Ben had not only survived the ravages of the
Blitz, but had also kept perfect time throughout.
On a number of occasions the microphones in the
belfry had picked up the sound of air raid sirens
and, in one particular instance in November 1943
the noise was such that it provoked consternation
among some listeners, who mistook the sirens for
their local air-raid warning. By 1944, the number
of flying bomb attacks had increased to such an
extent that it was considered advisable to suspend
live transmission of the bells for security reasons,
to prevent the sound of the explosions broadcast
with the chimes over the air giving the enemy an
advantage in locating their targets. Accordingly,
from 16 June 1944, although the clock continued
to chime and strike as usual, direct transmission of
the bells was discontinued. Up until this time the
sound of the bells had always been broadcast to

listeners directly from the microphones in the belfry, but for the time being, for the only period in the history of British broadcasting, the chimes were reproduced from a studio in the cellar of Broadcasting House where gramophone records of the bells were synchronised with the time. Although the recordings had been produced to the highest possible standard, obviously they were not of the quality which is available today. That they were recordings was obvious, and many listeners outside London feared that their beloved clock had been lost for ever through enemy action, despite the assurances which were given. However, the use of records proved to be short-lived, as live transmission was restored less than three months later on 8 September 1944, when it was considered that there was no longer a threat from flying bombs. And, needless to say, the broadcasts by the BBC have remained live ever since.

On the evening of 9 December 1944, shortly after the clock had chimed 10.45, the hands of Big Ben came to a standstill. Although it was feared that enemy action had been responsible, it transpired that the clock had suffered one of the few mechanical failures to occur during its long history. The pendulum suspension spring, a piece of very thin steel which secures the pendulum to its suspension bracket, had cracked and broken after eighty-five years of flexing continually for twenty-four hours a day. It has been suggested that the spring might have been weakened by the shock from the air raids three and a half years earlier. A new spring was fitted within a few hours, and although the clock was going by the following afternoon, the replacement spring required some 'running in'. This involved re-regulating the clock, and as a result it did run erratically for a little while, being replaced on the radio for the next few days by the Greenwich Time Signal.

At 9.30 on the evening of 24 April 1945, as the war in Europe was drawing to a close, the Ayrton Light was relit by the Speaker of the House, Colonel D. Clifton Brown. *Hansard* recorded the event as follows:

MR SPEAKER: If I might make a slight interruption in the proceedings at this stage I would remind the House that in peace time it was the custom that the lantern light above Big Ben always shone out, after sunset, in order to show that the House of Commons was at work. For five years, seven months and twenty-three days, this light has been extinguished. When I press the switch beside the Chair as I am about to do now, our lantern light will shine once more.

HON. MEMBERS: Hear, hear.

MR SPEAKER: In doing so I pray that, with God's blessing, this light will shine henceforth, not only as an outward and visible sign that the Parliament of a free people is assembled in free Debate, but, also, that it may shine as a beacon of sure hope in a sadly torn and distracted world.

I will now turn on our lantern light.
HON. MEMBERS: Hear, hear.

Just six days later, on 30 April, a small ceremony
was held in the Commons to mark the switching
on of the clock lights. At 10.15 p.m. the Speaker
threw a switch and once again the dials shone out
against the dark London sky, much to the delight
of the cheering crowds who had gathered below to
watch in Parliament Square.

Surely the most joyous news ever heralded by Big
Ben was the announcement of Victory in Europe on
8 May 1945. After the clock struck three that
afternoon, Winston Churchill, experiencing what
was probably the greatest moment in his life, and
hardly able to contain his emotion, delivered the
glad tidings that, in Europe, the war was at an end.
He suggested that people should relax for a few
days before sparing no effort to secure victory in the
Far East. That evening the clock tower was floodlit
and at 9 p.m., as Big Ben's last stroke faded away,
King George VI broadcast a message to his subjects
around the world. Finally, as Big Ben struck
midnight, the hour of total victory on 14 August
1945, the twelve majestic strokes were followed by
the quiet voice of the recently elected Prime
Minister, Clement Attlee, who announced calmly
that, at last and on every front the war was over.

It would have been impossible for the clock
tower to have remained undamaged under these
circumstances, and although some repairs were

carried out during the war they were mainly intended to be of a temporary nature. Due to the severe economic restraints which followed, a thorough overhaul of the clock and permanent repairs to its tower would not be undertaken until the mid-1950s. There can be no doubt that the Great Clock of Westminster played a vital part in maintaining the nation's spirit during the Second World War, the reassuring sound of the bells probably providing as great a boost to the morale of the British people as the speeches of Winston Churchill. On reflection, it is very gratifying to recall that throughout the six long years of the conflict, and despite being subjected to the full fury of the Blitz which seemed to threaten the clock's very survival, Big Ben maintained perfect time and was not stopped on so much as one occasion as a result of enemy action.

9

Great Tom Takes Over

During Big Ben's long and distinguished history there have been very few stoppages due to mechanical failure – little more than a broken spring or a snapped cable, with the clock being returned to duty within a matter of hours. There have been a few rare cases when maintenance or cleaning has required the clock to be stopped for some days, or even a week or two; for instance, in 1915 it was taken out of service for about a month for a clean up and in 1923 the clock was stopped for a fortnight so that an overhaul of the mechanism could be carried out. On only two occasions has it been necessary to take the clock out of service for a long period in order to undertake a programme of extensive maintenance.

By the early 1930s the strain of keeping time over London continually for three-quarters of a century was beginning to take its toll, and it was becoming obvious that a major overhaul would soon be necessary, which would require the clock to be out of action for some considerable time. Early in 1934 the BBC was told that the overhaul was to be carried out in the spring of that year and that, consequently, the bells would remain silent and be unavailable for broadcasting. The Westminster Clock had just celebrated its tenth anniversary as a regular broadcaster and the chimes were now established as a well-loved feature of the radio schedule with an audience stretching around the globe. The BBC felt that the sound of Big Ben would be much missed during any prolonged absence, and so the producers at Broadcasting House set about finding a suitable replacement to give the time signal over the air. An obvious choice was the clock of St Paul's, the cathedral church of the diocese of London. It stands at the top of Ludgate Hill in the heart of the City and is surrounded by streets with ecclesiastical associations: Amen Corner, Creed Lane and Paternoster Row. There has been a church on this site since long before the Norman Conquest, the original Saxon cathedral having been founded during the very early part of the seventh century. The present building is the third to occupy this position and is Sir Christopher Wren's masterpiece, having been completed in about 1710 after the previous cathedral was destroyed in the Great Fire. Steeped in history, St Paul's Cathedral has long been at the very heart of the spiritual life of the City of London. The north-west tower houses a magnificent ring of twelve bells cast at Loughborough in 1878. They were presented to the cathedral by various City livery companies, the tenor, weighing 3 tons 2cwt, was given by the City

Corporation. In the south-west tower is the bourdon bell, Great Paul, cast at Loughborough in 1881. At almost 16¾ tons, it is the heaviest bell in Britain. Raising it to the belfry 125ft above ground level was a massive task, undertaken by a detachment from the Royal Engineers. It is sometimes known as the 'Recall Bell', having been rung to call the City apprentices back to work after lunch, and is still sounded for five minutes at 1 p.m. every weekday. Most importantly, immediately below Great Paul is the cathedral clock, a first-class timekeeper.

Towards the end of the nineteenth century, the authorities at St Paul's were faced with the need to replace their ageing and rather cumbersome machine in the south-west tower. Impressed with the remarkable accuracy of the Great Clock at Westminster and knowing Lord Grimthorpe to be the designer of its movement, Gregory, the Dean of St Paul's, approached him for his advice. As usual, Grimthorpe was very enthusiastic and set about drawing up a specification for a new clock; this was constructed to his design by John Smith & Sons of Derby and installed in the south-west tower of the cathedral in 1893. The general construction bears many similarities to that of the clock at the Houses of Parliament, featuring a two second pendulum and, of course, the by now indispensable Grimthorpe double three-legged gravity escapement which makes for such excellent running. The clock is also known by the name of its hour bell, in this case Great Tom. Although the movement is of a similar size to that at Westminster the dials are somewhat smaller, being 17ft in diameter and featuring gold-coloured hands and markings against a black background. The previous clock had just two dials, facing south and west, but when the present clock was built a third dial, facing east, was added; there is no dial facing north. The hours are denoted by Roman numerals, including the traditional IIII in the four o'clock position, and the minutes are shown in arabic numerals at every quarter-hour.

Originally the clock was wound by hand daily – a task which took about thirty minutes – but in 1969 some modifications to the mechanism were made by John Smith & Sons, who continue to maintain the clock. Since then the going train has been wound automatically and the chiming and striking mechanisms are directly driven by electric motors and therefore require no winding. These changes have eliminated the risks associated with the use of massive driving weights – the very cause of the disaster which was to result in the destruction of the chiming mechanism in the clock room at Westminster just seven years later.

Despite having many similarities with Big Ben, the chimes of Great Tom are very different, featuring the 'ting tang' or 'ding dong' arrangement played on just two quarter bells. The history of Great Tom, the hour bell, has already been touched upon, for it is the very same bell that started life as

Edward of Westminster in about 1290 and was recast at the Whitechapel Bell Foundry during the early part of the eighteenth century when its weight was increased to the present 4 tons 12cwt 14lb. It hangs in the belfry above the clock room and is inscribed 'Richard Phelps made me 1716'. The bell sounds the note A flat. The quarter bells were cast at Whitechapel in 1707 and sound the notes A flat and E flat; this interval is played once for the first quarter, twice for the second quarter and so on, and is followed by the strokes of Great Tom on the hour. The tempo of the strokes is very similar to that of Big Ben.

Great Tom is considered to be the foremost clock in the City of London and the cathedral authorities were very pleased that it should be used to broadcast the time while the clock at Westminster was out of commission. They willingly gave their consent to the BBC who placed their microphones in the belfry. A number of tests were carried out and when the engineers were satisfied with the results, arrangements were made for the clock to go 'on the air'. As a prelude to the changeover, at 7.30 p.m. on Saturday 28 April 1934, the BBC broadcast a special edition of *In Town Tonight*, the weekly magazine programme which was to run until 1960. The programme opened with the chimes from Westminster and went on to give a brief history of the clock and the bells and to explain why Big Ben needed an overhaul. Finally, to prepare listeners for the sounds of Great Tom, the programme ended with the 8 p.m. strike from St Paul's. The cathedral clock began broadcasting regularly on 30 April.

The Great Clock at Westminster was stopped and taken out of service, the hands being set at twelve. Most of the work was to be carried out on the bells by the Whitechapel Bell Foundry. All the hammer-work was overhauled and two of the quarter bells were turned in order that their hammers could engage different parts of the surface. When Big Ben was delivered, just like most large bells, it had been supplied with a clapper suspended inside the bell from the collar. In change ringing, when a bell is rung, it is revolved by the pulling of a rope from below from its usual 'down' position through half a circle into the 'up' position and sounds when the clapper strikes the sound bow. But Big Ben is far too large and too heavy to be operated in this way – a bell of this size, no matter how finely balanced, if allowed to move would soon cause irreparable damage to the clock tower. In any case, clock bells remain stationary, being suspended from the girders and struck from the outside by their hammer. Consequently, there has never been any need for the clapper and it was taken down from inside the bell to lessen the weight on the collar. As there was insufficient space underneath the bell through which to remove the clapper, it was left on the platform beneath Big Ben, where it was to remain for the next twenty-two years. The opportunity was also taken to carry out a detailed inspection of the mechanism and to repair and replace a number of worn parts. Big Ben was under overhaul for about two months and Great Tom broadcast the time every day, making its final appearance on 2 July after which the microphones were removed from the belfry at St Paul's and the role of broadcasting was returned to Big Ben.

Considering the damage inflicted on the Palace of Westminster during the Second World War, it is probably true to say that the clock was lucky to survive. In 1954 the BBC were informed that Big Ben was to undergo a major overhaul, and that consequently the bells would not be available for broadcasting, probably for a period of about three months, the work being scheduled to start in the autumn of 1955. So the authorities at Broadcasting House investigated the possibility of using Great Tom of St Paul's once more, and again the cathedral was happy to oblige. On this occasion the outside broadcast engineers made some tape recordings of the clock, both on the hour and at each quarter, and these proved to be very useful as they allowed the sound engineers to demonstrate the sound of the bells to their colleagues.

As well as rectifying the damage to the tower, it was also considered necessary to undertake another major overhaul to both the bells and the mechanism. This was to be more extensive than on the previous occasion and would involve erecting scaffolding around the clock tower for the restoration of the masonry. Although the work had been planned for the autumn of 1955, the overhaul did not take place until 1956, by which time the newly rebuilt House of Commons had been functioning for some years. As it was felt that the noise from erecting the scaffolding might interfere with the broadcasting of Big Ben, arrangements were made to broadcast Great Tom before the clock at Westminster had been taken out of service. The BBC engineers duly installed their microphones in the belfry above the cathedral clock, and the *Radio Times* for 1–7 July carried a special feature entitled 'Great Tom takes over from Big Ben' which gave a brief history of the cathedral clock and compared the two hour bells. This was followed at 8.45 p.m. on Monday evening, 2 July, by *Big Ben and Great Tom*, a 15-minute documentary on the Home Service broadcast direct from both clock towers and introduced by John Snagge at Westminster and Wynford Vaughan Thomas at St Paul's. After the programme, Big Ben was broadcast for the last time before handing over to Great Tom at midnight on the Light Programme. Although it was estimated that the work on Big Ben would take about three months, the absence from the air was likely to be considerably longer, to allow for the erection and dismantling of the scaffolding.

The clock was now very nearly one hundred years old, and so it was decided to make a thorough inspection of the bells and hammerwork. All four quarter bells were lowered so that repairs could be made to their collars. The hammerwork

1. Edmund Beckett Denison, by Spy in *Vanity Fair. (Palace of Westminster)*

2. Charles Barry, by Henry William Pickersgill. *(Palace of Westminster)*

3. The belfry, showing Big Ben with the hammer mechanism
and two quarter bells. *(Palace of Westminster)*

4. One of the minute hands removed for examination.
(Palace of Westminster)

5. Cleaning the clockface.
(Palace of Westminster)

6. Behind one of the great dials. *(Palace of Westminster)*

7. The clock tower during the Blitz, showing damage to the south dial and the belfry area. *(Palace of Westminster)*

8. Winding the going train. *(Palace of Westminster)*

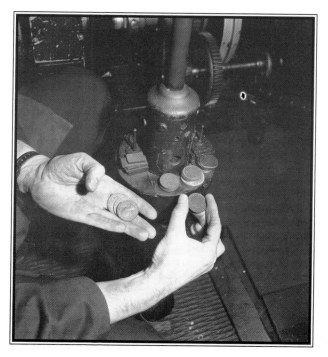

9. Pennies
on the
pendulum.
*(Palace of
Westminster)*

10. George Airy.
(National Maritime Museum)

11. Edward Dent.
(National Maritime Museum)

12. The clock room, showing the mechanism of the Great Clock.
(Palace of Westminster)

13. The Greenwich Time Ball in the 'dropped' or resting position,
Flamsteed House. *(National Maritime Museum)*

14. The clock of St Paul's on the south-west tower of the cathedral.
(Peter Macdonald)

was inspected and returned for repair to the Whitechapel Bell Foundry, and, for the only time since its installation ninety-eight years earlier, Big Ben was removed from its suspension so that the collar could be dismantled and inspected. With the bell now away from its usual position, it was possible to remove the clapper which had lain on the wooden platform beneath the bell since the previous overhaul in 1934. With the hammer having struck the bell in the same spot continually for almost a century, some consideration was given to turning it once more, in order to allow the hammer to fall on a different part of the surface. However, it was felt that this might affect the tone, which by now, of course, was universally recognised, and so the bell was replaced in its former position so that today the hammer strikes the very same spot which it has struck for almost one hundred and fifty years. The platform beneath the great bell, which had been added at Airy's suggestion in the early 1860s to protect the chamber from damage should the bell shatter, was lowered by about 18 inches, the finial on the spire was dismantled and regilded, and all openings in the roof, lantern and belfry were fitted with wire mesh panels in order to keep out the all-intrusive pigeons that had caused so much damage over the years. Again, a number of repairs to the mechanism were carried out.

At the beginning of the overhaul it had been hoped to have the clock available for the most important of its official duties, preparing the country for the two-minute silence on Remembrance Day; but as the work progressed this grew increasingly unlikely. Unfortunately, this target was missed by just a few days, resulting in Big Ben's only absence from the ceremony since its inception in 1920. On 14 November, just three days later, *The Times* reported that the overhaul was complete, and that the clock should start the same day and be on the air by the end of the month. Although the Great Clock had returned to service by the middle of November, it had been decided not to let Big Ben take up radio duties until the scaffolding around the clock tower had been removed, which, as the newspaper report had indicated, was hoped would be by the end of that month. The friendly 'ting tang' of Great Tom had been on the air since the beginning of July and the clock was proving very popular with listeners; indeed, the BBC gave serious consideration to retaining Great Tom on the Light Programme and confining Big Ben to the Home Service as soon as that clock became available for broadcasting, thus making for an easy identification between the national wavelengths. The authorities at St Paul's were delighted that the cathedral clock should be heard permanently over the air, but the proposal was not implemented as it was felt that Big Ben represents Britain and somehow gives 'authority' to the BBC. The scaffolding was taken down from the clock tower during December and Great Tom made its final broadcast at midnight after close-down on Saturday 22 December on the Light Programme. Big Ben returned to the air at 8 a.m. the following morning, Sunday 23 December, also on the Light Programme, thus making the Westminster chimes available for Christmas and, of course, for New Year's Eve. With the scaffolding removed and the beautiful stonework returned to its former glory, the Great Clock stood proudly over Westminster as it approached its centenary. As Big Ben was now giving the time on the Home Service and the Light Programme, the micro-phones were removed from the belfry at St Paul's and Great Tom returned to its usual duty as the foremost timekeeper in the City of London.

The clock at St Paul's Cathedral had proved to be a most reliable understudy during its two periods of broadcasting, but both occasions had been due to planned programmes of maintenance for Big Ben, and consequently Great Tom could be made available well before it was needed. However, Tom's next spell of broadcasting was to come without warning, and like a shot out of the dark. On Thursday 5 August 1976 at 3.45 a.m., the most serious breakdown in the history of the Great Clock occurred in the clock room at Westminster. While chiming 3.45, metal fatigue had caused the massive chiming weight, by far the heaviest of the three, to run wild, destroying much of the chiming mechanism and leaving the chimes silent for many months. Such was the devastation that it was feared the clock might never chime again. The BBC were informed that Big Ben had stopped and scheduled broadcasts were replaced with the Greenwich Time Signal until further notice. Fortunately, by carrying out some very rudimentary repairs, it was found possible to start the clock by about four that afternoon – little more than twelve hours after the disaster. It would also have been possible for the clock to strike the hours (although without the chimes), but as it was feared that there could be a similar fault with the striking mechanism it was decided to leave the clock going but silent, at least until the striking train had been inspected very thoroughly.

So, once again, the BBC were to look for a replacement to give the time on the air, and for the third time they approached the authorities at St Paul's Cathedral, who as usual, were very happy to oblige. Although the damage to the mechanism in the clock room at Westminster was catastrophic and the glorious chimes would not be heard for nine months, not only had it been possible to get the clock going on the very afternoon of the disaster, but also for most of the time while the chimes were unavailable, the clock would be striking the hours. Consequently, it was possible to retain Big Ben on the air for the hourly strike, which was broadcast most usually on Radio 4, while using Great Tom mainly for the quarter hours, which were broadcast almost exclusively on the World Service. It had been hoped that

Big Ben would be striking within a few days of the breakdown, but at noon on Monday 16 August the Great Clock was stopped to allow for a thorough inspection of the striking machinery. It seems that this is when Great Tom was prepared for his appearance on the radio, for the next morning *The Times* carried a photograph showing engineers from the BBC setting up some microphones in the belfry at St Paul's. Big Ben was started again at midday on Friday 27 August with the hourly strike in operation and over a period of several months both clocks were 'on the air', although it was necessary to silence or stop Big Ben on some occasions as work progressed. The exact schedule is uncertain but of the national networks, Great Tom was certainly heard striking the hours on Radio 3. It was the cathedral clock's longest period of radio broadcasting, extending for nine months from August 1976 until the beginning of May 1977. After this the microphones were removed from the belfry at St Paul's and they have not been needed since.

Although not so well known as the clock at Westminster, Great Tom has also had an interesting and varied career, and like Big Ben has a number of official duties to perform. In September 1939 at the beginning of the Second World War, during which church bells were to be rung only in the event of an invasion, the chimes were taken out of action by disconnecting them from the clock mechanism, so that during the war years the clock only struck the hours. Great Tom had a narrow escape in September 1940 when an unexploded bomb penetrated about 20ft into the ground a short distance from the clock tower. The cathedral was evacuated and although the clock kept going it remained unwound until the bomb had been removed by the disposal squad about three days later. By then the going weight had dropped to the full extent of the cable and the clock had stopped due to a lack of winding. This was the only occasion when the clock was stopped due to enemy action. The cathedral received two direct hits during the war, both of which caused considerable damage, and many other explosions occurred nearby, but St Paul's remained standing and the clock kept going. Indeed, it was often the only public clock in action over a large area of the city. The quarter chimes were restored at the end of hostilities in May 1945 and have remained in use ever since.

Throughout its history the clock has proved to be very reliable, for although there have been a few stoppages due to minor failures, it has never suffered a major mechanical breakdown. Whether Great Tom ever struck thirteen at midnight we shall probably never know, but it is recorded that on the morning of 21 November 1935 the clock struck 11.00 at 10.30. The cause of this aberration was not discovered and the clock went on to strike correctly at the hour. It is the city's first clock, and forms a part of ceremonial occasions. Great Tom tolls on the death of a member of the Royal Family, a Bishop of London, a Dean of St Paul's and a Lord Mayor of London during his term of office. Although Great Tom has not been used to broadcast the time signal for more than a quarter of a century, the clock has sometimes been heard in the background 'on the air' more recently, when there have been special services at St Paul's or ceremonies in the City.

St Paul's Cathedral is now approaching its tercentenary and a major refurbishment is under way in order to return the building to its full splendour in preparation for this notable occasion. This is a lengthy operation involving the restoration of both the exterior and the interior of the cathedral and it will take some time to complete. During part of 2003 and 2004, with both the north-west and the south-west towers hidden by scaffolding, the clock has been taken out of service. It is hoped that this part of the work will be complete by November 2004, when Great Tom should be striking the hours over the City once more.

Of course, the hour bell does not have the volume of the Great Bell of Westminster and it can easily be drowned by the continuous noise of passing traffic which may be heard from the cathedral steps. For anyone wishing to hear the clock strike, the best sound is probably obtained from slightly further away. On three occasions Great Tom has proved to be a worthy understudy to Big Ben on the air, and no doubt would be so again, should the need arise.

10

Big Ben Clocks up a Century

The completion on 31 May 1959 of 100 years of
almost unfailing service by the Great Clock of the
Palace of Westminster was a significant milestone
in the history of horology, as it marked the
culmination of a century of outstanding performance by a triumph of British design and craftsmanship, and one which many had supposed could
never be built. The clock was a magnificent piece
of horological engineering, the first public clock
ever to maintain really accurate time and setting a
standard which has never been surpassed, while
placing British clockmaking at the forefront
throughout the world. During its long and
distinguished career, the clock had become
established not only as a national treasure – a
greatly loved part of Britain's heritage – but also as
the nation's most authoritative timepiece, to which
all other clocks are compared. Copies of its gravity
escapement, which makes for such precise
timekeeping, had been fitted to most other turret
clocks; and the music of the bells, known
originally as the Cambridge quarters, was by then
world famous. Almost since the inception of radio

broadcasting the Great Clock had given the time signal over the airwaves and the clock tower had long been regarded as the symbol of Britain. In more recent years the chimes, the 'signature tune of the British Empire', had proved to be a great inspiration to both service personnel and civilians at home and overseas during the Second World War. With such an illustrious past, the opportunity to mark the Great Clock's 100th birthday could not be passed over and a number of events were scheduled to mark the occasion.

First, it was thought appropriate that some permanent commemoration should be produced to mark the centenary and it was decided that this would take the form of a commemorative inscription. This was to be set into a stone in the base of the northern wall of the clock tower where it could be clearly seen and read by passers-by in Bridge Street. The stone was carved during that summer and bears the following inscription in letters of Gothic script:

1859–1959
This stone commemorates the Centenary of
Big Ben and the Great Clock of Westminster

It would have been inconceivable, given the location of the clock and the history of Westminster, for this momentous occasion not to have been officially marked by Parliament, and so as the Great Clock struck eleven on the morning of

Wednesday 3 June 1959 a ceremony to commemorate the anniversary began in New Palace Yard.
Taking their seats on the platform that day were
the Prime Minister the Rt Hon. Harold Macmillan
MP, the Speaker of the House William Morrison
and his chaplain, the Lord Chancellor, the
Minister of Works Hugh Molson, the Lord
Chamberlain and the leaders of both the Labour
and Liberal Parties. Also present were members of
both Houses of Parliament and representatives of
organisations concerned with the study and
manufacture of clocks and bells, including David
Buckney, Chairman and Managing Director of E.J.
Dent & Company. As the last stroke of Big Ben
faded away, the Speaker's chaplain read the
following prayer:

> Let us thank God for them who in generations
> past dedicated their gifts of design and skill and
> industry to raise aloft this tower and therein to
> set up this Bell. Thanks be to God.
> Let us give thanks that, surviving the dangers
> of war, to ever widening circles across the world
> this Bell has sounded forth; symbol of stability
> in time of peril, symbol of unity in time of
> peace, recalling day by day the great traditions
> which we have inherited in this place. Thanks
> be to God.

After the prayer, the Speaker addressed the
assembled company:

My Lords, Ladies and Gentlemen,

We have met to celebrate the hundredth anniversary of Big Ben. The name is properly applied to the great bell which strikes the hour; so called after Sir Benjamin Hall, Mr Molson's predecessor in office a century ago. We are glad to see among us today Major Monteith, the great grandson of Sir Benjamin Hall, the original 'Big Ben'. By popular usage the name has come to be used not only for the bell but also for the clock.

The Great Clock is somewhat like our Parliamentary Constitution in that, though it was born in controversy and wrangling, yet it keeps excellent time and serves us admirably. It was designed by that (sometimes irascible) genius, Mr Denison QC, later Lord Grimthorpe. The clock mechanism, exclusive of the bells, weighs five tons: so it is not the kind of timepiece that a man wears on his wrist. The central feature of the mechanism is the escapement devised by Denison and now known to horologists, the world over, as the 'Grimthorpe double three-legged gravity escapement' – a standard feature of most great public clocks. It may be noticed that this escapement is double like our bi-cameral Parliament, that it is three-legged, like the 'Three Estates of the Realm'. Furthermore, that it relies on gravity, or the pull of mother earth, for its correcting influence – mundane, practical and thoroughly British. It works.

This contrivance of Denison's has a certain great merit. External influences such as wind pressure on the fourteen foot long minute hand, are not communicated to the pendulum. No matter what gales may rage up there, the pendulum, with a bob of four hundredweights at the end of its thirteen foot shaft, beats its two second swing unconcernedly, unaffected by what is happening outside. Exact time is thus maintained. Human beings cannot maintain the impassivity of bronze or iron, but it is not inappropriate to say that in all the storms of the centuries that have beat upon us, the pulse of our Parliament has maintained a certain steadiness and regularity of 'Order' in its proceedings.

After much contention, the manufacture of the clock was entrusted to Mr Dent, a famous clock maker of the time. The firm which he founded has maintained the clock, under contract, over the century. The extraordinary accuracy of this purely mechanical clock is a remarkable tribute to their zeal and care and also to the skill of the Victorian workmen who cut the gearwheels and other parts with implements of the time and to their successors who have carried on the good work. I am glad to see here Mr D.P. Buckney, the Chairman and Managing Director of the firm. He is the great-grandson of the original Mr Dent, the original clockmaker.

Big Ben proper, the great hour bell, had a genesis as stormy as the clock. The first bell cast broke when struck by its ponderous hammer. It was recast into a new bell which now hangs in the tower. The new bell, too, cracked when struck with the heavy hammer. The crack was expertly treated, the bell given a quarter turn, so that the blow should fall at right angles to the weak part, the weight of the hammer reduced to four hundredweights and this is the great bell we hear today.

Not only we. Thanks to the invention of wireless and the British Broadcasting Corporation, the voice of the great bell is now heard all over the inhabited earth. It was during the last war that the sound of its strokes attained a peculiar poignancy, especially during the time when we stood alone. No doubt Big Ben sounded somewhat differently to those that loved us and to those who hated us. To our friends in all countries it was reassuring. Even though at times there were the background noises of sirens and the gunfire of our artillery, its punctual boom said that neither Big Ben nor the nation was put off its stroke by those things. To those who were bent on our destruction I think it sounded otherwise.

It may be that the microphone, being so near the bell, picked up imperfections, such as the crack. Microphones are very revealing. It may be that the technical difficulties of broadcasting at that time, when wavelengths had to be synchronised, led to some distortion of the sound received. It seemed to me, in any case, in those days, when I heard the great thirteen and a half tons of metal struck by the four hundred-weight hammer, that the bell gave forth a harsh roar of defiance, and thereafter, a long reverberating growl, menacing ultimate destruction to our enemies.

Now Big Ben sounds down to us his mellow E natural, the voice of peace and goodwill. So may he sound to our children's children, generation after generation.

Immediately after the Speaker had concluded his address, he presented the Minister of Works with a wooden replica of the inscription which was to be carved into the stone and set in the base of the clock tower later that year to commemorate the anniversary. This replica has since been fixed on the wall of the clock room, where it may be seen by visitors.

Following the completion of the ceremony in New Palace Yard, the platform party was conducted the short distance from the Houses of Parliament to the Jewel Tower of the Palace of Westminster in College Mews to enjoy a preview of the special centenary exhibition which had been set up showing the history of Big Ben. The official exhibition was housed on two floors and featured an interesting and comprehensive display of many varied items concerned with the history of the clock, several of which were being shown for the first time. Viewing was available to members of both Houses of Parliament immediately after the ceremony and the exhibition opened its doors to the general public on the following morning.

As visitors approached the Jewel Tower, just outside the entrance they saw the original 6½cwt hammer which had been used for striking Big Ben in 1859, and which now resides in the clock tower. Once inside the entrance they were greeted by one of the original models of the clock tower which had been made by James Mabey, one of the gifted stonemasons who worked alongside Sir Charles Barry. It was a beautiful and extremely detailed model, and correct in every aspect. Its maker had taken every opportunity to become familiar with the intricate construction of the tower and he had obviously put his knowledge and observation to good use, as the model revealed itself as the work of a very skilled and experienced craftsman. On the wall of the exhibition was a large drawing of the clock's movement, reproduced full size to give visitors an impression of the scale of the mechanism, and to the front of this drawing was a series of patterns lent by Dent & Company which had been prepared for the casting of various parts. In a display panel were mounted portraits of the personalities associated with the building of the clock and its tower: Edward Dent, Sir Charles Barry, Sir Benjamin Hall and, of course, Edmund Beckett Denison. Also on show was an enlarged copy of Dent's contract for the maintenance of the

Great Clock. It had been signed by Elizabeth, Dent's wife, and at the time of the exhibition was still in force having twelve years left to run before the responsibility of maintaining the clock was to be taken over by Thwaites & Reed in 1971. Of particular interest were two working exhibits, one of which visitors were invited to operate. The first of these was an automatically wound clock, made by Messrs Dent and featuring the double three-legged gravity escapement. Shown running, the clock proved to be one of the most interesting exhibits, and demonstrated to visitors what a tower clock is like. The other working model was a display of the gravity escapement, which had been made especially for the exhibition by Major F.B. Cowan and Mr F. West of the British Horological Institute. Visitors were invited to wind up the going weight and to see the escapement in action. As the workings of this escapement are rather difficult to explain, the model illustrated its action perfectly, making it easy to understand. Other exhibits included the view of one of the clock faces taken from behind the dial, showing how it appears when it is seen laterally inverted, and a photograph of the famous pennies, which are used for regulating the clock, in place on the tray near the top of the pendulum. Also on show was the pendulum's original suspension spring, which had snapped in December 1944, and a model of the gas burners used to illuminate the dials at night before electricity was employed. The contracts for casting both the hour bells, first with Warner & Company at Cripplegate and then with Mears at Whitechapel were displayed, together with drawings of proposed elevations for the clock tower, the earliest of which dated from 1841.

On the floor above were further exhibits including some letters between Denison and Airy. There was also a section made up of contemporary references largely from *The Times* and other publications, including this amusing skit which appeared in *Punch* during November 1857 shortly after the first bell cracked:

To Disraeli

Big Ben is cracked, we needs must own,
Small Ben is sane, past disputation,
Yet we should like to know whose tone
Is most offensive to the nation.

A tape-recorded commentary dealing with significant details of the clock's history was played at frequent intervals and put out over a series of loudspeakers. Most appropriately, the music of the bells was relayed directly from the belfry in the clock tower every fifteen minutes so that visitors could hear the clock chiming and striking. The oak plaque which earlier that day had been presented by the Speaker to Mr Molson, the Minister of Works, was taken to the Jewel Tower to be displayed in the exhibition. The Royal Observatory loaned some extracts from the Astronomer Royal's reports regarding the performance of the clock. A template of the great bell was on show, and another attraction which proved to be very popular was a miniature set of the quarter bells which visitors could chime for themselves. There was a detailed description of the Westminster chimes showing how they had been devised, a portrait of their probable composer, William Crotch, and a photograph of the University Church of Great St Mary in Cambridge. There was a model showing how a large bell is cast, and this, together with diagrams of the moulds, was valuable in showing how Big Ben was made; another model showed how the belfry appears to a visitor to the clock tower. One particularly interesting exhibit showed quite realistically how the view over London and the Houses of Parliament appears to anybody looking out from the belfry.

A booklet *The Story of Big Ben*, the official guide written by Alan Phillips and published by Her Majesty's Stationery Office, was available at the exhibition. It gave the background to the building of the clock tower and told the history of the clock over those hundred years. Neatly presented and well illustrated, it made the ideal souvenir and probably filled in a few gaps for visitors to the exhibition. The centenary of Britain's most famous timekeeper was thus given the prominence it deserved, with the exhibition remaining open until the middle of September. It is to be hoped that the authorities at Westminster will arrange a similarly informative exhibition for the 150th anniversary in 2009.

A preview in the *Radio Times* announced: 'This week the BBC is celebrating the 100th birthday of one of its most famous broadcasters – Big Ben, the thirteen-ton hour-bell in the tower of the Palace of Westminster which every day marks the opening and the close-down of programmes.' And at 9.15 p.m. on the evening of 3 June, the very day of the centenary commemoration in New Palace Yard, the Home Service put out a special programme entitled *The King of Clocks*, a thirty-minute feature documentary written and presented by Alan Burgess. The programme approached the subject from a popular standpoint and consisted mainly of a commentary on the history of the clock and its place in British national and Commonwealth life, together with some sound effects illustrating the chimes and a number of recorded interviews, including one with Mr Buckney from Dent's.

As part of the centenary celebrations, the orb and shower of stars on the top of the clock tower steeple were illuminated by floodlighting. Although the clock tower had been floodlit on a few previous occasions, this was the first time that the pinnacle had been lit up, as earlier equipment did not have sufficient power to throw such a narrow beam of light to the required altitude. The clock tower was originally floodlit in September 1931 as part of the International Illumination

Congress. It was later lit for the Silver Jubilee of King George V in 1935, the Coronation of King George VI in 1937 and the Victory celebrations at the end of the Second World War in 1945. Beginning with the Festival of Britain in 1951, the clock tower was illuminated every summer, apart from in 1956 when the clock underwent its major overhaul and the tower was shrouded in scaffolding. Since 1964 the floodlighting has been switched on throughout the year.

Big Ben has always been popular in the United States and it comes as no surprise to discover that the centenary celebrations were not confined to Britain. In July 1959 *The Times* reported that a huge clock, to be named after Big Ben, was to be installed in New York's Grand Central railway station as a gift from an American horological firm. The newspaper described it as 'the biggest indoor timepiece in the world', its dial 15ft in diameter and its hour hand 4ft 9in long.

Considering the enduring popularity of the Westminster Clock, it is no wonder that a number of models have been produced. Of course, miniature versions are on sale in almost every gift shop in London, and some bear a good resemblance to the real thing. Over the years some working models have also been made, probably the most notable being 'Little Ben', which was erected originally outside London's Victoria station in 1892. It was manufactured from cast iron and stands about 15ft high. After more than seventy years of service, it fell into disrepair and was taken down in 1964 to make way for road improvements. The clock was missed by the many passengers travelling to and from Victoria each day, and after a lapse of seventeen years it was completely restored by John Smith & Sons of Derby. The clock has been fitted with a new electrically operated mechanism and a 1cwt bell which strikes the hours, an automatic cut-out silencing the bell between midnight and seven in the morning. The clock was reinstated by Westminster City Council in December 1981 on one of the traffic islands just outside the station. The cost of restoring Little Ben was borne by the French oil company Elf Aquitaine as a gesture of Franco-British friendship, and the clock bears the following inscription, a dry reminder of the difference in the time kept on each side of the English Channel:

LITTLE BEN'S APOLOGY FOR SUMMER TIME
MY HANDS YOU MAY RETARD OR MAY ADVANCE
MY HEART BEATS TRUE FOR ENGLAND
AS FOR FRANCE

Although the Great Clock at Westminster appeared to remain virtually unaltered after its first 100 years of operation, it had undergone a few developments and seen a few changes since being brought into service in the summer of 1859. First, the Ayrton Light which shines out from above the belfry when either House is sitting was installed in 1885. The original beacon, with directional visibility, could be seen just from west London, but the present light with its all-round visibility, was installed in 1892. The unsightly gas burners behind the dials were replaced by electric lighting in 1906. Electric winding (for the chiming and striking trains) was introduced in 1912, and in 1916, during the First World War, the Daylight Saving Act was introduced, advancing the time by one hour during the summer months and necessitating the clock to be stopped twice a year for adjustment.

Big Ben did not toll on the death of Queen Victoria, but it did toll on the deaths of three kings: Edward VII in 1910; George V in 1936; and George VI in 1952. The Great Clock had been associated with the annual ceremony at the Cenotaph on Remembrance Day since its inception in 1920, and from 1924 had achieved world wide recognition through broadcasting.

Looking back over that century, one wonders if any of those who were responsible for the design and construction of the clock could ever have foreseen the position which it would occupy in the nation's heritage 100 years later.

11

Mishaps, Curiosities and Breakdowns

Like so many things which we take for granted without appreciation, perhaps we only notice Big Ben when the hands have stopped. Once the clock had become established and people had begun to rely on its excellent timekeeping, generally speaking it was just a failure of the mechanism or some other stoppage which would bring it into the news.

The clock's strength lies in the sheer genius of its design and the rigidity of its construction, but its weakest points are probably its size and its exposure to the elements. For many years it was the largest clock in the world and it is not surprising, therefore, to find that there have been more stoppages due to bad weather and the thoughtlessness of careless workmen than have been caused by mechanical failure. The compensated pendulum and the gravity escapement ensure accurate timekeeping, even during extremes of temperature – both hot and cold. However, it has been in the severest of winters when temperatures have fallen to several degrees below freezing that an accumulation of snow forming on one of the clock faces has brought the hands to a standstill, and when layers of ice on the bell hammers have caused faulty chiming. Even so, bearing in mind the length of service which the clock has seen and the frequency of bitter spells, particularly during past decades, stoppages due to bad weather have been quite rare.

In February 1900 a particularly heavy snowfall caused the clock to stop for about eight hours. Although the weight of snow landing on one of the hour hands can be sufficient to slow it or bring it to a standstill, more often it is a drift of snow building up on the ledge beneath one of the clock faces which impedes the hour hand as it approaches the half hour and causes the clock to stop.

In the winter of 1928 the clock was again stopped by a heavy fall of snow and was out of action for several hours. Severe weather on 25 January 1945 caused the rubber bushes on the quarter bell hammers to freeze and muffle the chimes. At 9 p.m., listeners awaiting the main evening news on the Home Service heard the first quarter chime bell and then three or four 'thumps' from the bell hammers instead of the chimes, followed by the six pips of the Greenwich Time Signal. The announcer stated that because of a mass of ice freezing on the hammer mechanism Big Ben was not available and had been replaced by the pips. The situation had not improved in the morning and the 7 a.m. strike was also replaced by the GTS, but at 9 p.m. that evening Big Ben was back on the air. Just two years later, on 28 January 1947, the same problem occurred and at midnight listeners heard a few fragmentary notes of the chimes followed by one stroke of Big Ben, and then silence. The situation appears to have been resolved by the morning.

Snow caused further trouble on 13 January 1955 when the hands were brought to a stop at 3.24 a.m. due to drifts forming on the north and east dials. Small electric heaters have been placed just inside these two dials, which face the full fury of the winter's blast, and this measure has helped to reduce incidences of freezing in recent years. On 9 January 1968 snow was again responsible for stopping the clock when drifts on the faces brought the hands to a standstill at 6.28 a.m. The clock was going again at 10.10 a.m. It is interesting to note that on both occasions when the time of the stoppage due to snow (1955 and 1968) has been recorded, the minute hand was approaching the half hour where its progress would have been impeded by the freezing mass on the ledge beneath the clock face. The spring of 1986 must have been somewhat colder than usual, for at the beginning of March the rubber bush on the largest of the quarter bell hammers froze and muffled the chime. The following January another spell of severe weather caused the rubber bushes on all the quarter bell hammers to freeze, muffling the chimes.

As the nation's bell, Big Ben's most solemn duty has been to toll for a departed monarch. The bell was first required for this purpose in 1910 on the death of King Edward VII. As described earlier, Big Ben was originally fitted with a clapper which provides the usual method of tolling, but the proximity of the timber platform underneath the bell prevents any attempt to strike it by this means. A temporary modification was therefore made to the striking mechanism by Messrs Dent & Company and, with the chimes silent, this enabled the Great Clock to toll the bell automatically. The sound was muffled by the insertion of a leather pad between the striking hammer and the bell which softened the normal harsh metallic tone. The bell tolled on the morning of 17 May on the occasion of the removal of the King's body from Buckingham Palace and stopped as the coffin arrived in Westminster Hall for the Lying in State. It tolled again on the morning of 20 May as the Royal Procession left Buckingham Palace for Westminster Hall to escort the body of the King to its final resting place and ceased when the body left London for Windsor. This whole arrangement was found to work very well, since the tolling was completed without the slightest mishap. In February 1936 Big Ben tolled for the second time, on the death of George V. The earlier method of tolling seems to have been brought into use and, in any case, the clapper would not have been available as it had already been removed from the collar of the bell during the major overhaul in 1934. In February 1952 Big Ben tolled for the third time on the death of a king when George VI died.

On a few occasions, the status of Big Ben has been used to attract attention. In May 1928 *The Times* reported that a youth on holiday from Leamington Spa had challenged the Great Clock to a race at midnight, attempting to sprint across Westminster Bridge in less than 38 seconds, the time taken for Big Ben to sound the twelve strokes. He covered the 236 yards in 26 seconds, so he appears to have won the bet. On 11 June 1984, while the clock tower was hidden behind scaffolding as part of a two year cleaning prog- ramme for the whole Palace of Westminster, two Greenpeace activists scaled the tower in order to make an environmental protest. Perched in hammocks slung by the south face of Big Ben they displayed a banner reading 'Time to Stop Nuclear Testing'. After eleven hours they came down of their own accord. *The Times* reported that they were fined £20 each. On 20 March 2004, a day of protest against the Iraq war, in a stunt reminiscent of twenty years previously, two Greenpeace activists managed to evade security and scale the clock tower from where they exhibited a banner reading 'Time for Truth', in a protest against Britain's involvement in the conflict.

On 23 September 1936 while a gang of painters was decorating the inside of the clock tower and when they were working in the clock room, one of them leaned a ladder against one of the shafts which drives the hands, causing the clock to stop. The incident was reported in the *Daily Express*, which quoted the foreman as saying: 'I looked up to see the time and Big Ben had stopped. Of course, they blamed me for putting the ladder up. But how should I know? I'm no clockmaker.' How indeed? The shafts revolve silently and so slowly, once an hour, that they appear to be stationary. The clock had stopped at 8.47 a.m. but was going again by 10 a.m.

One of the more amusing incidents concerning Big Ben occurred during the evening of 12 August 1949 when starlings landed on one of the minute hands, slowing the clock by five minutes. It is not recorded how long the birds remained on their lofty perch, but although the clock was not available to broadcast at 9 p.m. it was back in service by midnight.

There have been times when the bells have sounded incorrectly or not at all, or been stopped through human error. On New Year's Day 1941, one of the notes was missing from the quarter chimes. The cause was not recorded, but the clock appears to have been working normally by the next day. On 3 June 1941 the clock was stopped again by human error. This was less than a month after the House of Commons had been destroyed in the bombing raid and the glass in the south facing dial of the clock tower had been blown away. Work had begun on repairing the dial, and a carpenter when going off duty for the day had left his hammer on a bracket near one of the hour driveshafts. At about 10.15 p.m. it fouled the mechanism and the clock stopped. As this was just a few weeks after the air raid, which it was supposed might have weakened the mechanism, it must have come as a great relief to discover the cause of the trouble. Big Ben was going again some twelve hours later.

On 18 July 1955 another mechanical failure silenced Big Ben but left the clock going. The rope which operated the striking hammer broke and the clock did not strike from 10 a.m. to 5 p.m., although the chimes sounded as normal.

On 28 May 1957, listeners awaiting the nine o'clock news on the Home Service were surprised to hear the announcer say: 'By now you should have heard Big Ben strike for nine o'clock, but something we don't quite understand has happened to Big Ben.' Something, indeed, had happened. A painter who had been working in the clock room had left a paint pot on one of the girders and it caught the counterweight of an hour hand, stopping the clock at 8.38 p.m., just twenty minutes before it was due to broadcast the 9 p.m. strike. Seemingly, nobody at Broadcasting House had been informed.

On the afternoon of 30 October 1961, anyone expecting to hear Big Ben striking 4 p.m. would have been puzzled at the silence which followed the chimes. A defect in the winding gear prevented the four strokes from sounding, but the clock was back to normal an hour later.

The nearest Big Ben has come to missing the New Year celebrations was on 31 December 1961. At midday snow on the northern face had slowed the hands by ten minutes but fortunately it was cleared by midnight so that the clock could strike in the new year.

On 30 January 1965, the day of Sir Winston Churchill's funeral, as the Great Clock chimed 9.45 a.m. the procession left Whitehall. Then, as a mark of respect, the bells were kept silent for the rest of the day and were not heard again until midnight.

In 1966 the Great Clock seems to have been prone to a few minor defects. On 18 February at 10 p.m. the clock chimed but did not strike – embarrassing as it would have been 'on the air' for the news at ten. The same thing happened at 11 p.m. The cause this time appears to have been a loose shackle in the striking mechanism. On 22 June the winding motor overwound the striking train, shearing half a tooth from a cogwheel in the process, so that just the chimes were sounding. The problem took some time to rectify as Big Ben did not sound until 6 p.m. the following evening. On 17 October the chimes were heard to miss a note on each quarter from 8.30 a.m. until 10.30 a.m. due to a disconnected rod. Finally, on 21 November a defect in the winding mechanism stopped the clock for about twenty minutes during the afternoon.

In January 1976 the bells were silenced for two days to allow for some decorating work to be undertaken in the tower, and during this time the clock stopped for about three and a half hours, although without any apparent cause. Could another painter's ladder have been responsible?

However, all these incidents, although inconvenient, were as nothing compared to the catastrophe that struck suddenly and without warning on the morning of Thursday 5 August 1976. This was to be the worst disaster in the long and distinguished history of the Great Clock, worse even than the cracking of Big Ben more than a hundred years earlier. At 3.45 a.m. the policeman on duty in New Palace Yard heard a muffled thud and noticed that Big Ben had stopped. He immediately telephoned the Engineer's Control Room to report the matter. The engineer on duty thought that probably one of the cables had snapped and that the noise which the policeman had heard was the sound of the massive weight landing on the sandbags at the bottom of the clock tower. His first act was to inform the BBC that the chimes would not be available for broadcasting and then he made his way up the steps to the clock room to investigate the cause of the trouble. When he opened the clock room door he was confronted by a scene of utter devastation, the like of which he could probably never have imagined, even in his worst nightmare. The bedplate had been broken in several places and much of the clock mechanism was reduced to a heap of useless metal lying on the frame, with broken gearwheels and shafts scattered around the floor. Small metal fragments were embedded in the walls and ceiling and there were some holes in the ceiling where larger pieces of metal had been forced through the timber and into the lever room above.

The engineer thought that a bomb must have been detonated under the clock frame and he summoned the Bomb Squad from the police station at nearby Cannon Row. The Bomb Squad were soon on the scene and climbed the tower to the clock room. Although shocked at the scale of the devastation, they quickly dismissed the idea of any explosion, for although some of the windows had been smashed, the detonation of a bomb would have caused such a sudden rise in the air pressure that the glass would have been blown out. After making an extensive search of the clock room and the belfry and finding nothing suspicious, they concluded that the destruction had been caused entirely by mechanical failure. Before even considering the possibility of any repair, it was deemed necessary to obtain a record of the scene in the clock room for the parliamentary records and an official photographer was summoned from the Department of the Environment. It was also necessary to inform the Resident Engineer of the Palace of Westminster John Darwin, the Speaker of the House of Commons George Thomas (later to become Viscount Tonypandy) and the Chairman of the Commons

Accommodation and Administration Committee Robert Cooke.

Anyone entering the clock room on that fateful morning would have resigned themselves to the probability that the Great Clock would never go again. The clock room had always been dominated by the stately tick produced by the swing of the pendulum every two seconds and now it was silent, as though the very heart of London had stopped. Standing among the debris, the prospect of the clock ever being returned to its former self must have seemed an impossible dream. The chiming barrel had been thrown across the room to land on the wooden bench below, which it had smashed. The chiming mechanism had almost completely disintegrated and both the going and striking trains had been damaged. The famous Grimthorpe escapement had been twisted to such an extent that it was now useless. However, even in this apparently hopeless situation one could distinguish two pieces of good fortune. Firstly, the pendulum and the pendulum cock, although so near to the ruined escapement, had been left unscathed and, secondly, in a cupboard in the clock room there was a spare escapement. Many years previously, the original escapement had been damaged and a new one fitted. The original had been repaired and kept as a spare. While it must have seemed unlikely that the clock could ever be completely restored to its original condition, there was now just a glimmer of hope that it might go again.

Later that morning, two heavy duty jacks, each capable of raising a load of 3 tons, were brought up to the clock room in order to support the weight of the broken bedplate, and throughout the day work continued on clearing the debris. At about 4 p.m. it was decided to see if the clock would start. After a few adjustments, the pendulum was given a very gentle push and everybody in the clock room held their breath. Then their hearts must have filled with joy as the escapement was engaged and they heard the imposing and familiar tick. Once again Big Ben was going, and not only going but telling the time with his usual accuracy. This must have lifted the spirits of all involved because now, little more than twelve hours after the disaster which had damaged so much of the mechanism, it had been possible to start the clock. This was a tribute not only to the Victorian engineers who had built the clock, but also to the devotion and determination of their twentieth-century colleagues who were now being inspired by it. Although it would have been possible for Big Ben to sound the hours that very afternoon, because the striking train is so similar to the chiming train it was decided to keep the clock silent until tests could be carried out on the striking mechanism.

Once the clock had been restarted a discussion was held in the clock room to consider the possibility of a full repair of the mechanism with the complete replacement of the chiming train. Present at this meeting were Robert Cooke Chairman of the Accommodation Committee, Geoffrey Buggins

Managing Director of Thwaites & Reed the clock maintenance contractor, and John Darwin the Resident Engineer of the Palace, on whom fell the responsibility of restoring the clock to full working order. Mr Cooke stressed the need for the full restoration of the clock, drawing attention to its special importance as the symbol of Britain and an integral part of the Houses of Parliament. He also reminded the others that Her Majesty the Queen was due to visit the Palace of Westminster in almost exactly nine months' time to receive the Loyal Address of both her Houses of Parliament on the occasion of her Silver Jubilee. His committee considered it essential that Her Majesty should be welcomed by the full chimes of Big Ben as she arrived at noon on 4 May 1977. Mr Buggins took a more cautious approach, advising that although his firm had the expertise and the facilities to undertake the massive task of repairing and reconstructing the clock, he estimated that the work would take at least fifteen months, and so would not be complete until November 1977. Additionally, outside the meeting several 'philistines' were muttering that it might be time to scrap the antique clockwork movement and replace it with a modern synchronous electric motor. Mr Darwin felt that it might just be possible to meet the date of May 1977, and after further deliberations this was adopted as the target.

The cause of the disaster appeared to be the fracture of the chiming flyfan arbor (driveshaft).

The flyfan acts like an airbrake, governing the speed with which the chiming barrel revolves. With the shaft broken, all air resistance had been lost and the system ran wild until the massive weight hit the sandbags at the bottom of the tower. The broken chiming arbor was sent for examination to the National Physical Laboratory (NPL) at Teddington, where it was confirmed that the break in the shaft was due to metal fatigue. The striking arbor was also examined at the NPL and found to contain fatigue cracks, so the clock remained silent until a new shaft could be made and fitted.

For the ten days since the disaster, Big Ben had been absent from the airwaves, and so on 16 August the BBC installed some microphones in the belfry of St Paul's Cathedral and, once again, Great Tom was broadcasting the time signal. At noon on 27 August, just twenty-two days after the disaster, the striking mechanism was brought into use and Big Ben was again heard sounding the hours over London.

The main question which arose was whether it would be practical to repair the clock. Why waste time, money and effort on such a colossal undertaking if further weaknesses might cause another disaster in the future? As the fault in the broken chiming arbor appeared to radiate from the inside, it was conceivable that similar faults on other parts could remain undetected until it was too late. It was therefore decided to carry out a very thorough radiological examination. This was undertaken by the Non Destructive Testing Section of the United Kingdom Atomic Energy Research Establishment (AERE) at Harwell. The work took place in the clock room, mostly when the clock was stopped for the change back to Greenwich Mean Time during the weekend of 23 to 24 October. On this occasion the clock was stopped for an extended period of thirty-three hours, from noon on Saturday until 8 p.m. on Sunday. The scientists were therefore able to work through the night, and early on Sunday morning they discovered extensive cracks in the gears which drive the striking flyfan arbor. This was extremely serious as a failure in these gears could have caused a disaster on the scale of that which had destroyed the chiming train the previous August. So, as a precaution, striking was suspended immediately. A new set of gears was made and fitted very quickly, and having been silent for just a week the Great Clock was striking once more on Monday 1 November.

After the delays caused by the examination of the movement for further defects, the possibility of meeting the target date of May 1977 appeared to be receding. One further problem was the scarcity of original plans and drawings of the mechanism. As any documents which might have been kept in the Resident Engineer's office would have been destroyed when the House of Commons was bombed in 1941, searches were made in the Public Record Office, the Old Royal Observatory at

Greenwich and the National Maritime Museum, but unfortunately nothing of any consequence was found. The situation was not helped by Denison's rather cavalier attitude towards engineering drawings, which he considered to be quite unnecessary. This was a great inconvenience, as about one third of the movement needed to be replaced and most of the parts would have to be made from scratch. The official investigation into the failure was carried out by scientists at the Materials Applications Division of the National Physical Laboratory and their report was published by the Institution of Mechanical Engineers. This confirmed that the disaster had indeed been caused by metal fatigue in the chiming fly arbor. The researchers also concluded that the arbor had actually broken during the 3.30 a.m. chime, at the end of which the train was stopped, as usual, by the locking lever. This lever was also discovered to contain a fatigue crack, and when the train was unlocked for the 3.45 a.m. chime the barrel accelerated to a such a speed (about 1,600 revolutions a minute instead of the normal rpm) that it broke off the head of the locking lever. There was now nothing to stop the chiming barrel running out of control and wrecking the mechanism.

The absence of the sound of the quarter chimes on the radio was much regretted and the BBC were anxious to know whether they would be available for New Year's Eve. Unfortunately, this would not be possible, although Big Ben was broadcast as usual to strike in the new year, but without the chimes. Since the middle of August Great Tom had been giving the time signal, mainly on the World Service but also on Radio 3, while the strike of Big Ben was heard Radio 4.

The discovery of hairline cracks in the striking flyfan gears during the radiological examination in October required that each newly manufactured component should be similarly examined by the Harwell team prior to being accepted. The Great Clock had now been operating for some months with the movement supported rather precariously on the two hydraulic jacks and with no chime; it could not be allowed to continue in this fashion. Of course, although silent it is still a beautiful clock; but with no chime it lacks its crowning glory, rather like a blackbird with no song or a rose without a scent. Somehow it *had* to be restored.

Finding a contractor willing to undertake the enormous task of rebuilding the clock was proving to be extremely difficult. Of those who had been approached, quite understandably, none could guarantee to meet the target date of May 1977. Eventually, the work was entrusted to Messrs Thwaites & Reed, which had maintained the clock since 1971. This long-established company, which had bid unsuccessfully over a century earlier for the tender to build the Great Clock, was now in a unique position as it was completely familiar with its workings and was to achieve a splendid effort in restoring it. Before commencing work, one important factor to be taken into account was that since it was a priceless antique, great care had to be taken to ensure that the clock's appearance remained the same, or as near as possible, to the original. One exception to this requirement was that whereas the original gearwheels had been made out of cast iron, their replacements were to be manufactured from gunmetal, as this would make for greater durability. Obviously, the manufacturing work was not without its difficulties, but, bearing in mind the scale of the operation, it progressed very rapidly and was virtually complete by the end of March 1977.

The work of reconstructing the mechanism began in April and was conducted, as far as possible, with the clock running. However, it was necessary to stop the clock for a week at the end of the month to allow for the completion of the task. There was still much to do and most of the remaining work, such as aligning and bolting the new chiming train section of the bedplate, which quite apart from the running of the clock was important for the appearance of the inscription, and removing the two jacks which had supported the frame for the previous nine months, could only be carried out when the clock had been stopped. Moreover, there was no possibility of requesting extra time as this was the last week before the Queen's visit. Thanks to the heroic efforts and enthusiasm of all concerned, in particular of John Vernon, the Technical Director of Thwaites & Reed and John Darwin the Resident Engineer of the Palace, the task was completed and on Saturday 30 April the clock was started. The bells were tested on Sunday and at noon on the following Wednesday, 4 May, the chimes were restored and the Great Clock was returned to full service having triumphed over seemingly impossible odds. With Big Ben sounding the full range of chimes, the microphones were removed from the belfry at St Paul's and the Great Clock of Westminster resumed its rightful place on the air.

Ten years later, during the changeover from BST to GMT on 24 to 25 October 1987, some cracks were discovered in the striking flyfan bracket, necessitating its renewal. The hour bell was out of action for a week, during which time the chimes were either broadcast without the hourly strike, or the clock was replaced entirely over the air by the Greenwich Time Signal.

And in 1990 the great bell was to be silent once again. Metal fatigue had developed in the striking hammer arm and in March *The Times* reported that Big Ben would remain silent 'for three months' while the arm was replaced. This may seem a very long time to manufacture one replacement part, but in fact there was no hourly strike for much longer. The new hammer arm was fitted on 29 August and the clock resumed striking. Since March it had just sounded the quarter chimes and on the hour Big Ben was replaced on the radio by the Greenwich Time Signal.

Interestingly, although the hour bell was unavailable for as long a period as during the overhaul in 1956, no attempt appears to have been made to broadcast Great Tom. On 1 August, while the hour bell was still silent, the clock stopped for three hours for no apparent reason. The BBC considered that the new hammer arm had altered the tone of the bell and refused to broadcast it for several weeks, finally relenting on 22 December just in time for Christmas and the new year.

On 23 January 1994 the clock stopped at 9.30 p.m. for more than three hours. Again, no cause could be found. On 30 April 1997 an escapement bearing tightened itself, stopping the clock from 12.12 p.m. for about forty minutes. This was slightly amusing as there was to be a General Election the next day, and the stoppage of Big Ben was believed by some to be a most ominous portent. On 11 November 2002 while Big Ben was broadcasting the 11 a.m. strike on all national wavelengths, the microphones picked up the sound of some young visitors being conducted around the belfry. This was considered to be most inappropriate at such a solemn moment and the BBC received complaints from several listeners.

Finally, during the 12.45 a.m. chime on 29 April 2004 the locking lever on the chiming mechanism gave way through metal fatigue. The clock continued going and striking but the chimes remained silent for ten days while a replacement part was manufactured and fitted. During this time the clock was replaced over the air by the pips until the chimes were restored on 9 May. Although no damage had been caused to the mechanism on this occasion, the failure could have been serious and the new lever was subjected to a radiological examination prior to installation, a similar inspection also being undertaken on the corresponding section of the striking mechanism.

It seems that mechanical failures have been quite rare, and apart from the disaster in 1976, have soon been rectified. With the present level of attention given to the clock, there is every reason for confidence that this admirable record will be maintained in the future.

12

A Glorious Moment

Just before twelve on the morning of Wednesday 4 May 1977 Her Majesty Queen Elizabeth II arrived at the Royal Palace of Westminster to receive the Loyal Address from both Houses of Parliament on the occasion of the Silver Jubilee of her accession to the throne. This was only the third occasion on which loyal addresses have been presented by Parliament to celebrate a royal jubilee. The first was in 1897 when both Houses presented addresses to Queen Victoria at Buckingham Palace to celebrate her Diamond Jubilee and the second was in 1935 when both the Lords and the Commons presented addresses in Westminster Hall on the occasion of the Silver Jubilee of King George V and Queen Mary. This year's ceremony was also to be held in the ancient Westminster Hall, built originally by William II (William Rufus) in the eleventh century; saved from the disastrous fire in 1834 which had destroyed most of the Old Palace, it had been the scene of many royal occasions during more than 900 years of British history.

For an hour before the royal party arrived the band of the Scots Guards had played selections from Elgar, Coates and Vaughan Williams and as Her Majesty and His Royal Highness the Duke of Edinburgh entered the Hall at noon, the chimes of the Great Clock rang out clearly and joyfully for the first time in nine months, followed by the twelve deep strokes of Big Ben. As the last stroke faded away the Queen took her seat before the assembled company which included HM Queen Elizabeth the Queen Mother, HRH the Prince of Wales, Princess Anne and most members of the royal family, together with the establishment of the Lords and Commons. Also present on this occasion was an array of judges, bishops, diplomats and other dignitaries.

The Loyal Address on behalf of the House of Lords was read by the Lord Chancellor, Lord Elwyn-Jones, and that on behalf of the House of Commons by the Speaker, George Thomas MP. Representatives of both Houses presented the Queen with bound copies of their address, after which Her Majesty rose to give her reply. The Queen thanked the Lords and the Commons for the kind words expressed in their addresses. She said that while the Jubilee was principally a time for reflection, it also provided the opportunity to look forward. Then to a fanfare of state trumpeters of the Household Cavalry she handed copies of her speech firstly to the Lord Chancellor and then to the Speaker. Finally, the Lord Chancellor led the singing of the National Anthem and the whole assembly rose to give a tumultuous 'Three cheers for Her Majesty'. To have returned the Great Clock to its former splendour in time for this was a magnificent achievement. The ceremony marked the beginning of nationwide celebrations which continued throughout the summer in every city, town and village in Britain.

Barely nine months earlier, to those who had surveyed the unbelievable damage in the clock room, the prospect of the clock ever being restored to its former glory must have seemed an impossible dream. But now, thanks to the skill and devotion of all who had been charged with the enormous task of rebuilding the mechanism, that dream had been fulfilled.

During the long months when the clock had been under repair, the authorities at Westminster had received many enquiries from listeners around the world expressing their concern and even offering their services if this would do anything to help restore the beloved chimes to the airwaves. Furthermore, John Darwin, the Resident Engineer at the Palace and responsible for managing the rebuilding of the shattered mechanism in time for the royal visit, had been required to give several interviews on radio and television both at home and overseas in an attempt to satisfy the demand for information. His efforts in restoring the clock are justly remembered on a small plate commemorating the reconstruction of the chiming mechanism which has been affixed to that end of the bedplate in the clock room.

In view of the continuing public interest in the clock and the considerable amount of concern which had been expressed while it was out of action, the decision was taken to mount an exhibition telling the story of the catastrophe. The exhibition was held in Westminster Hall and as well as describing the background to the disaster, it was illustrated with many pictures, and featured a display of some of the damaged parts of the mechanism. It proved to be very successful as it was seen by several thousand visitors, initially at Westminster and subsequently at other locations around Britain where it appeared on tour. As the sound of the chimes had been particularly missed 'down under', the exhibition was shipped out to Australia, where it was just as popular.

With the clock now fully restored to its original condition, in the early 1980s the Property Services Agency (PSA), the department then responsible for maintaining government buildings, decided it was time to embark upon a thorough cleaning and restoration programme for the whole of the Palace of Westminster. This was to be a multi-million pound operation which would extend over several years, but with completion due before the end of the decade. The main purpose was to restore the stonework to its original condition and to remove the need to undertake further renovation until well into the twenty-first century. In March 1983 scaffolding was erected around the clock tower in preparation for the restoration of the stonework and the dials, which was to take about two years. Unlike the mechanical overhauls in 1934 and 1956 when most of the work had been undertaken in the belfry and the clock room, on this occasion there was no need to stop the clock as repairs were not required to the mechanism. Most attention was to be paid to the masonry and the repairs turned out to be quite extensive, requiring more than 100 cu. ft of Clipsham stone, brought in from Rutland quarries. Some of the ironwork also needed a certain amount of attention and the regilding of decorated surfaces used some four thousand books of gold leaf. When it came to repainting, the PSA turned to the Royal Commission on Historical Monuments for advice concerning the decoration of the carvings which surround the dials, and this resulted in a return to the original red, blue, green and gold colour scheme. The original colour of the metalwork surrounding the dials was uncertain and samples taken from the Latin inscription below one of them revealed that although the two most recent applications had been in black, underneath were layers of white, red, white again, cream and gold – some choice. The Commission advised that a shade of blue might be suitable, but in the end it was decided to continue with black as this had been well known for many years since its introduction in 1934 and was now recognised around the world from television images.

Despite the radiological testing of much of the mechanism carried out as a result of the breakdown in 1976, there was some concern over the condition of the hands and their central bearings as these had been inaccessible since the clock was built over 125 years previously. With the clock tower now surrounded by scaffolding, the opportunity was taken to make a thorough inspection of these parts. Even at this stage it did not become necessary to take the clock out of service as each of the four dials was examined separately, with the clock going and showing the time on the other three faces and with the bells sounding as usual. All the hands were removed in turn, and tested radiographically for flaws. They were found to be in remarkably good condition, but it was decided to renew the central bearings which pivot the hands as these were beginning to show some signs of wear. This was the final stage of renovating the clock tower, which had taken just over two years to complete.

On 5 June 1985 the Speaker of the House, Bernard Weatherill MP, performed a small ceremony at the south face of the clock when he tightened the nut which holds the hands in position. This marked the completion of the work and the official unveiling of the clock faces which had been hidden from view by the scaffolding and plastic sheeting during the restoration. The 'ceremonial nut' which was used on this occasion has been retained and forms part of the small display which may be seen by visitors to the clock tower. This facelift for the clock tower won the

PSA the City of Westminster's Heritage Award for 1986. The clean-up had removed years of grime caused by soot and smog. Fortunately, the air over London is much cleaner now than it was in the past and it is anticipated that the clock tower will not require another major overhaul during the next fifty years.

As the end of the twentieth century approached, so people's attention became focused on the arrival of the third millennium. The anticipated event almost gave birth to a new industry, and with so many recent developments in technology and communications it was obvious that it would be celebrated simultaneously around the world – a veritable global party – like the new year but perhaps a thousand times louder. For many the idea of a new millennium appeared to hold an almost magical significance, as if it were the dawning of a new age. Of course, opinions vary as to the timing of the event. The present era is measured from 1 January AD 1, therefore the third millennium began on 1 January 2001 after the passage of 2,000 calendar years. Popularly, however, it was celebrated one year earlier. Those living in Far Eastern longitudes, in New Zealand and some of the pacific islands for instance, where the time is twelve hours or more ahead of GMT, considered themselves to be among the first to pass into this new age and there were celebrations across each continent as the hour of midnight circled the globe. In Britain many cities have their own way of marking the arrival of the new year. In Edinburgh, for instance, which is considered to hold the foremost celebration, the One o'Clock Gun is always fired on the stroke of midnight, and in London, of course, there could be no better way of welcoming a new century than with the chimes of Big Ben.

About a year beforehand it was announced that the new millennium would be greeted in London by a spectacular firework display to be held along the banks of the Thames, with floats on the water. Well before midnight on New Year's Eve 1999 the area was thronged with thousands of revellers eager to mark the occasion. Big Ben has never failed to strike in the new year (although on New Year's Eve 1976 the chimes were absent); in fact, the idea of greeting the new year without the glorious chimes would be unthinkable and in August 1999 a plan was put forward to produce a spectacular multicoloured light show on the dials of the Great Clock on New Year's Eve. The proposal entailed the lights behind the faces switching on and off in time to the music of the chimes at midnight and the projection of com-mercial logos on to the clock face. Quite properly, the authorities at Westminster immediately rejected the idea of incorporating any commercial dimension; not only did they feel that this would lower the status of the clock, but they also considered that as a part of British national heritage it should remain above advertising. In the end the idea of the light show was abandoned and the Great Clock was left alone to be itself – a symbol of Britain. It was broadcast at midnight as usual, no doubt to the accompaniment of fireworks, and then again at noon on New Year's Day at the start of the New Year's Day Parade in London. The Great Clock at Westminster had now been keeping time for the nation in three different centuries – the nineteenth, the twentieth and for just a few hours of the twenty-first.

13

A Look to the Future

The 150th anniversary of the Great Clock is fast approaching, and it is to be hoped that the authorities at the Palace of Westminster will take the opportunity to mark this historic occasion, possibly by staging another exhibition. Throughout its long and distinguished career, this masterpiece of Victorian horology has continued to assert itself as Britain's national symbol while maintaining its enviable position as the country's most authoritative clock, and it is essential that the highest standard of maintenance be employed to ensure its survival for future generations.

Although failures of the mechanism have been very rare, nevertheless the clock is a machine and as such is liable to break down. The disaster in 1976 could not have illustrated this more clearly and it demonstrated the need for some preventive measures to be taken in order to avoid another catastrophe in the future. From what had occurred, it was obvious that the integrity of the clock could not be left to the brief time afforded when routine inspections are carried out three times each week during the winding operation or when the clock is stopped twice a year in the spring and autumn for the change to or from Summer Time. The radiographical non-destructive testing of parts carried out by scientists from the Atomic Energy Research Establishment at Harwell during the changeover from British Summer Time to Greenwich Mean Time in October 1976, just a few months after the disaster, had revealed defects in thirteen castings, all of which had to be replaced. This had shown the wisdom of undertaking such an examination as it had revealed several hidden faults which, if left unattended, might not have been discovered until it was too late. It was therefore proposed to undertake a non-destructive examination every ten years to allow for defects which are presently too small to be revealed, but which might extend into fatigue cracks in the future. Even this programme of periodic radiographical examination was considered insufficient to safeguard the clock against all contingencies.

It was felt that something was needed on a day-to-day basis in order to protect the mechanism and its surroundings in the event of a sudden failure. So the National Physical Laboratory was approached and requested to design and manufacture a device which would cut in immediately to stop the mechanism from running out of control, should there be a fracture in one of the flyfan arbors or the bevel gears. The commission was arranged by John Darwin, the Resident Engineer, who stipulated two conditions: first, that the device should be fail-safe and not subject to accidental operation; and, second, that it should be concealed within the mechanism so as not to detract from its historical appearance. For the new device to be fail-safe it would have to be more reliable than the very clock itself, and what could be more reliable than the Great Clock had proved to be over more than a hundred years? A number of designs were proposed but these were rejected mainly on the grounds that they would not blend in with the character of the clock.

After many months of research and experiment in the NPL workshops an ingenious device was designed by John Furse, a senior engineer, and the prototype was fitted to the chiming train during the changeover from BST to GMT in October 1977. The device is wonderfully simple, being entirely self-contained and purely mechanical in operation. It consists of a centrifugal ball clutch which is driven by gearing directly from the hand winding wheel on the chiming barrel. During chiming, at the barrel's normal speed of rotation the ball is held in position under gravity, but were the barrel to accelerate, at a given speed the ball is thrown out by centrifugal force, the clutch engages and operates the brake which grips the rim of the winding wheel, bringing it safely to rest. The fail-safe device was installed initially just to the chiming train. During the years which followed the major breakdown the device was tested on two separate occasions while the clock was stopped for the changeover to or from BST, and it was found to work well each time. It came into operation, stopping the weight, which had been lowered almost to the sandbags at the base of the weight shaft, within a few inches. In 1981 a similar device was fitted to the striking train. It must be appreciated, however, that these precautions represent the very last line of defence against disaster, to be applied automatically, when all other measures have failed. Regular maintenance and periodic radiographic testing of the high risk components for symptoms of metal fatigue must constitute the main strategy for keeping the clock in good shape.

At the time of the clock's construction, Britain was undergoing a scientific and mechanical revolution, while great strides were also being made in the fields of engineering and natural history. In 1859, the very year when Big Ben struck his first hour, Brunel completed his masterpiece, the monumental Royal Albert Bridge taking the Great Western Railway beyond Devon, across the Tamar and into Cornwall, and in the same year Charles Darwin published his revolutionary *Origin of Species*. Although electric clocks had been developed in about 1840 it was still a mechanical world; sound recording, the telephone, radio and television lay decades into the future, as did the development of flying, and the prospect of the 'digital age' – of microchip computers and mobile telephones – would have seemed unbelievable even to the most prescient scientist.

In the intervening period, the science of horology has changed dramatically, almost beyond recognition. The traditional clockwork design was superseded firstly by electric movements and then by quartz, and most recently by radio controlled devices, all of which have had consequences for the maintenance of mechanical turret clocks. Even the second, the very unit of time, is not what it was. Until 1960 the second was defined as a specific fraction (1/86400) of the mean solar day. (Each minute contains sixty seconds, each hour sixty minutes and each day twenty-four hours; therefore each day comprises 60 x 60 x 24 = 86400 seconds.) Now we are in the age of atomic time and this is based on counting the cycles of a high frequency electrical signal which is kept in resonance with an atomic transition. The fundamental unit of atomic time is the Systeme International (SI) second which is reckoned as the duration of 9,192,631,770 periods of the radiation corresponding to the transition between two hyperfine levels of the ground state of the cesium-133 atom. The accuracy claimed for some of these clocks is one second in many thousands of years, but this excursion into the world of atomic timekeeping is way beyond the scope of this book. It is obvious from all this that the craft of clockmaking is no longer based on astronomical observation and the skill of the craftsman but on the laws of physics and atomic science.

For more than the first hundred years of its life the Great Clock at Westminster was maintained by its manufacturers E.J. Dent & Company, whose responsibility included the winding and regulation, routine maintenance and changing to and from Summer Time. The company also undertook to attend at any time, day or night, should a problem occur. This arrangement worked well, but it could not forsee the impact of the new technologies. As the number of clockwork mechanisms being constructed slowly dwindled, so it became more and more difficult to recruit clockmakers with sufficient expertise in the maintenance of turret clocks, and in 1970 Messrs Dent asked to be relieved of their contract. In fact the decline in trade was so severe that the company went out of business shortly afterwards. In 1971 their place was taken by Thwaites & Reed, a very well respected company which, as mentioned earlier, did an excellent job in rebuilding the mechanism after the catastrophe in 1976. Thwaites & Reed were to look after the clock for the next thirty years, because since 2002 the maintenance has been carried out by the Parliamentary Works Directorate. Today no clockwork turret clocks are being built and consequently there is very little need to train a new generation of clockworkers in their maintenance; as with so many of Britain's traditional crafts and industries, there is little demand and skills are being lost. While there now exists the technology to carry out X-ray examinations of vulnerable components in order to reduce the risk of mechanical failure, remedial steps need to be taken to ensure that sufficient skill is available to rectify such a failure in the years to come.

The developments in technology also mean that the role of the Great Clock has changed. In the middle of the nineteenth century, at the time when the clock was conceived, public clocks were essential for the regulation of domestic life. Almost every town and village had one, usually erected on a church or civic building from where it could be easily seen and clearly heard by the local population. It provided a valuable service indicating the time, and was regulated by frequent comparison with a sundial. To many town dwellers and those working in the fields the chimes of the local clock provided their only indication of the time. With the advent of radio broadcasting during the early part of the twentieth century and the introduction of the Greenwich Time Signal and Big Ben on the air, an accurate time check was available throughout the country. However, as most domestic clock mechanisms were clockwork, they required regular winding and adjustment at frequent intervals, and for this the listener would rely on the broadcast time signal.

At the beginning of the twenty-first century the time is everywhere available. A quartz wristwatch may be purchased very cheaply and provides a level of accuracy which would have been unthinkable even a few decades ago, requiring alteration just twice a year when the time is advanced or retarded. Time is on display virtually everywhere in our modern homes, not only on clocks (usually quartz) but also on the cooker, the video recorder, the telephone answering machine and the computer, to name just a few. This must explain, in some part, why the chimes of the Great Clock are not broadcast so frequently as they were in the past. The clock has become more ceremonial, rather than practical.

The original purpose of the Great Clock was to sound the hours over London to within a second of the time. It represented the very pinnacle of turret clockmaking and accuracy, which it still maintains and which has never been surpassed on a turret clock. Its designer and builder could never have foreseen the place their clock would come to occupy in the national consciousness. Of course, there can be no comparison between the mechanical workings of a clockwork movement and the electrical signals generated by an atomic resonator, yet despite all these advances in horology and physics the Great Clock remains Britain's most authoritative timepiece. It is the very heartbeat of the capital, loved by Londoners and visitors alike, and extensively photographed – one only has to stand near the Houses of Parliament to see the many tourists snapping at the clock tower, wishing, perhaps, that they could take it home. In some ways they can, for quite apart from their photographs, a recording of the bells is available on compact disc and one internet site even offers to bring the sound of the chimes to your computer every fifteen minutes. Recently a 'sound artist' has proposed setting up an attraction which would relay a montage of noise, modified and made more interesting by certain techniques, from the clock room to a chamber near the base of the clock tower. While some may regard these latest ideas as little more than gimmicks, they do demonstrate the enduring appeal of the clock.

Appendix I

A VISIT TO THE CLOCK TOWER

Although the clock tower forms part of a royal palace and is not generally open to the public, it is possible for those with sufficient enthusiasm and the energy to climb the three hundred or so steps to arrange a visit to see inside the clock room and the belfry. When the tower was built its main purpose was to house the clock mechanism and the bells and so little thought was given to the admittance of visitors. For this reason conditions inside the clock tower are rather spartan and the ascent is by means of a narrow staircase, which can be hard work. Consequently, a visit would not be suitable for the elderly or infirm and young children are not admitted. In addition, due to the confines of space, parties have to be limited to about sixteen persons. Regrettably, another factor which presently has to be taken into account is the issue of security, unfortunately, recent events have shown that this cannot be overlooked. Nevertheless, tours of the clock tower are available, and can be arranged through members of either the House of Commons or the House of Lords. It is usual for intending visitors to apply through their MP, whose office will make the necessary arrangements.

Tours start on the half-hour, and it is important to be on time in order to arrive in the belfry for the hourly strike. Those with a few minutes to spare can stroll over Westminster Bridge and admire the clock from across the river, where it may be seen and heard in all its beauty. When passing the clock tower on returning towards the Palace, it is possible to read the inscription on the commemorative stone which was set in the base of the tower to mark the centenary of the Great Clock in 1959.

Once through the security check, it is customary to meet the guide near the foot of the clock tower. After making a brief introduction, he will escort the visitors into the tower and up the staircase. The staircase occupies an oblong space and consists initially of short flights of steps separated by right-angled turns. This first part of the climb is a little austere because the bricked up windows shut off a number of little-known prison cells. On the first floor of the tower is the parliamentary prison, a room which can be approached only through the apartments of the Serjeant-at-Arms. Its purpose was for the detention of members of either House who had been rude or noisy during debates. In theory a member could be detained for the remainder of the parliamentary session but in practice he would be held only overnight. This cell has not been used for a very long time, in fact the last member to have the pleasure of a night's accommodation in the clock tower was Charles Bradlaugh who, in 1880, as an atheist refused to take the Oath of Allegiance.

After about a hundred steps a halt is usually made to give the party a break while they visit a room which houses a small display of photographs and artefacts relating to the clock, including the original hammer which was used for striking Big Ben. The remainder of the climb is usually taken a little more slowly as the staircase becomes tighter and more difficult to negotiate and most visitors start to notice certain leg muscles which are not normally apparent! After almost a further one hundred and ninety steps the staircase opens on to an inner gallery which runs behind the clock dials. Set about 5ft inside this gallery, the walls are painted brilliant white in order to afford the greatest possible reflection. At this range the dials seem enormous and it is only when one is able to walk around behind them that their size and beauty can be appreciated. The dials were designed by Pugin, who unfortunately did not live to see the completion of the clock, and are fashioned out of opal glass mounted in cast iron frames. Each dial weighs 4 tons and contains 312 panes of glass. For much of the Second World War the dials contained nowhere near that number of panes since every face received some damage through the effects of bombing, with the south dial being completely blown out during the Blitz in 1941, although remarkably the hands were not damaged. As a temporary measure whitened boards were inserted into the broken parts of the dials, after which the defects were virtually invisible from ground level. The driving shaft for the hands may be seen extending through the wall from the clock room, together with its heavy counterpoise which is situated just inside the dial. On a bright day particularly, it is fascinating to watch the movement of the minute hand from such a close range. The dials are always illuminated at night and initially this was by means of gas jets which also provided enough heat to prevent a build up of ice on the hands, except during the very severest of winters. It was not until 1906 that electric lighting was installed, removing the need to despatch a man to the gallery every evening in order to light the gas. This too generated sufficient warmth to stop the forming of ice on the hands, but in 1957 the original tungsten bulbs were replaced by a cold cathode lighting system which made for greater efficiency but with virtually no heat escaping to protect the hands small electric heaters were provided behind the north and east dials. This method of illumination has now been superseded by banks of low energy fluorescent bulbs and these may be seen on the walls just inside the dials. Upon leaving the space behind the dials, a few further steps lead to the clock room which is set within the square bounded by the dials and is, of course, the very heart of the machine.

The clock room is a quiet and well-ordered place and is completely dominated by the stately tick produced every two seconds as the pendulum engages the escapement. Most visitors are surprised at the sheer size of this room which is about 36ft long and 16ft wide and would wonder how there could have been any dispute regarding the fitting of the mechanism within it. The difficulty arose in getting the mechanism as close as possible to the centre of the area inside the dials and as this was obstructed by the walls of the central core it became necessary to mount the flyfans on long vertical shafts extending almost to the ceiling, rather than in the conventional manner on horizontal shafts behind the mechanism. It was this unavoidable modification to the original design which was to contribute directly to the great catastrophe in 1976.

The appearance of the mechanism, which is 15ft long and 5ft wide, is rather like that of a flatbed printing press. From the front, just behind the safety railings which are designed to prevent spectators from getting too close and being caught up in one of the massive gearwheels, it can be seen that there are three interlinked sets of gears and drums. The small one in the middle is the going train which does exactly what its name implies – it keeps the clock going. At each end there is a larger set, the one on the left being the striking train and the one on the right the chiming train. Clearly visible along the front of the bedplate is the inscription naming Frederick Dent as the clock's builder and Edmund Beckett Denison as its designer and giving the year of manufacture, 1854. (This inscription also appears along the back of the bedplate.) Just beneath it on the front is the small plate which shows the year of fixing the mechanism in the clock room, 1859.

Overhead are the driving shafts for the clock's hands, aligned with the four points of the compass. High above are the two flyfans, and the cables which operate the bells may be seen running up from the mechanism through the ceiling and into the belfry above. Slightly more difficult to make out are the cables dropping from the mechanism to the weight shaft far below. For those who wish, the guide will take them behind the mechanism to view the tray near the top of the pendulum on which are placed the pennies used to regulate the clock.

Quite suddenly the solemn tick is interrupted by a loud click. Some visitors seem startled and may be inclined to wonder if something has gone wrong within the mechanism, but this is 'the warning', to use its technical name, which sounds two minutes before the chimes are due to enable anyone working on the clock to get clear before the huge cogs start to turn. After the warning there is what seems like two very long minutes before the giant wheels begin to revolve and the flyfan starts to whirl round, making a terrific 'clattering' noise. At quarter to the hour each of the four quarter bells is chimed three times and although their muffled sound can be heard in the clock room, together with the thuds of the hammers as they are operated by the cams which control the five quarter bell ropes, it is the sound of the flyfan which drowns everything else. But in a short while this noise dies away as the fan slows down and the quiet and solemn atmosphere returns. Before leaving the clock room there is time to have a look at the oak board bearing the 'Members' Prayer' – the words written to the music of the chimes – and to see the wooden replica of the commemorative plaque which was set in the base of the clock tower to mark the centenary of the Great Clock.

When the three-quarter chime has finished, there are just another forty-four steps to the belfry. The belfry marks the climax of the tour, for it is here where Big Ben reigns in majesty attended by his four quarter bells. At stormy times the wind roars through the Gothic tracery and the rain can sweep in, so one hopes for a calm day. On arrival most visitors are surprised at the size of the bells which are suspended from the huge gantry. After a few moments visitors should have recovered from the effects of the long climb and be ready to appreciate the stunning views which may be had and to pick out some of the well-known landmarks – Westminster Abbey, Buckingham Palace and the London Eye for instance. Spectators are separated from Big Ben by a wire mesh barrier which surrounds the platform constructed underneath to protect the tower should further damage occur to the bell.

Overhanging the Great Bell is the hammer mechanism, and the massive hammer itself rests about 9in away from the bell. The dulling of the surface struck by the hammer is clearly visible, and the guide will point out the famous crack and the slot designed to prevent it from spreading any further, but it may be difficult to read the inscriptions around the skirt from this distance. It will be noticed that the largest of the quarter bells which sounds the note B has been provided with two hammers. During the third and fourth quarters this note ends one bar and starts the next and a single hammer would be unable to operate at the required interval, hence the fifth cable from the chiming train. Above the bells in a corner of the ceiling are the microphones which carry the sound of the chimes around the world. The guide will point these out and usually ask the party to keep quiet while the bells are sounding as they might be 'on the air'.

Unlike the clock room there is no warning click in the belfry and so, all of a sudden, all thoughts are drowned as the quarter bells chime their full sequence. At the quarters it is the first note which marks the time, but on the hour the chimes start about twenty seconds early to allow their music to fade sufficiently before before Big Ben strikes. The quarter bells appear quite loud, but Big Ben is, of course, very much louder. Then, exactly on the hour, the giant bell hammer is released and strikes the Great Bell. This is very dramatic and visitors often place their hands over their ears, but even so, it is not as loud as one might expect and most people adapt to it. When Big Ben is being struck the whole belfry appears to shake from the tremendous vibration, and at this range the tone seems very harsh and metallic, subtly different from the mellow and more pleasing sound which may be heard from Bridge Street or from across the Thames. The hourly strike, which marks the end of the tour, is truly magnificent and is well worth the effort involved in climbing the clock tower. To stand in the belfry at the Palace of Westminster when Big Ben is striking must be every clocklover's dream.

Finally, after a more leisurely descent of the staircase, the party returns to the base of the clock tower where the guide leaves them with a brief factsheet about the clock and memories of a really wonderful experience.

Appendix II

THE WHITECHAPEL BELL FOUNDRY

Bellfounding is an ancient craft. The basic principles have remained much the same through the ages – the beautiful Bellfounders' Window in York Minster, for example, depicts a medieval founder using techniques which are little changed to this day. For centuries the foundries scattered throughout the length of Britain catered for the needs of the many new churches which were being built, but as the number of new churches declined so the bell foundries dwindled. By 1900 there were about a dozen in existence, including John Warner & Sons of Cripplegate who had cast the original Big Ben and the four quarter bells for the Great Clock in 1856 and who were to stay in business until about 1920. Since the cessation of founding operations by the Croydon-based firm of Gillette & Johnson in 1950, just two remain: John Taylor & Company of Loughborough in Leicestershire and the Whitechapel Bell Foundry in London. Both these concerns have a long pedigree and can be proud of the many fine bells which they have produced and it is fitting that they should have survived. Taylors, for example, have the honour not only of casting Britain's heaviest bell, Great Paul, the bourdon bell of St Paul's Cathedral in London made in 1881, which at nearly 17 tons hangs in the south-west tower, but also of producing the fine ring of twelve which was installed in the north-west tower in 1878. They also manufactured the second heaviest bell in the country, Great George, the bourdon bell of Liverpool (Anglican) Cathedral which weighs 14¾ tons and hangs in the Vestey Tower. Interestingly, this bell, which was cast in 1938, was not named after England's national saint but in memory of King George V.

But it is with the foundry at Whitechapel in the heart of London's East End that we concern ourselves here. The Whitechapel Bell Foundry was established near Aldgate in 1570 during the reign of Queen Elizabeth I and is recognised to be the oldest manufacturing company in the United Kingdom. It can trace an uninterrupted line of descent of over four hundred years from Robert Mot, master founder in the late sixteenth century, whose stamp depicting three bells forms the basis of that which is still imprinted today on all tower bells cast at Whitechapel. Mot was one of a line of master founders going back to Robert Chamberlain who flourished in Aldgate from about 1420, some of whose bells still survive. The foundry can therefore claim a continuous succession spanning almost six hundred years.

In the early part of the eighteenth century the foundry made much progress mainly through the introduction of change-ringing, the new art in which a peal of bells is rung through many permutations, as this became established first in London and then in other major cities such as Norwich and Cambridge. It was during this period that the foundry underwent considerable expansion under the direction of Richard Phelps, who in 1716 recast Great Tom, the hour bell of the clock at St Paul's Cathedral, which at over 4½ tons was, at the time, one of the heaviest bells in the country. The company moved to its present site, a former coaching inn called the Artichoke in the busy Whitechapel Road, in 1738 in response to the growing demand for bells both from home and abroad. In the same year the foundry cast the famous Bow Bells for the church of St Mary le Bow in Cheapside and in 1752 made the equally famous Liberty Bell. Following its arrival in America the bell was reported to have cracked at the first stroke and was recast locally. This proved to be unsuccessful and so it was recast again – it is this second recasting, which is also cracked, which now hangs in Independence Hall, Philadelphia. Before the end of the century the foundry had achieved an international reputation for its fine bells, helped no doubt by London's position as a major seaport.

In the nineteenth century, firstly under Thomas Mears, the foundry cast its heaviest bells. This began with the recasting in 1834 of another Great Tom, this time belonging to Lincoln Cathedral. It weighed over 5 tons and was the largest bell to have been cast in Britain for over one hundred years. In 1845 the foundry cast Great Peter of York Minster. At 10 tons it was the heaviest bell which had ever been made in Britain. In 1927 it was recast by Taylors of Loughborough when its weight was increased to more than 10½ tons and it is now the fourth heaviest bell in the country. Then, in 1858 and by now under the direction of George Mears, the foundry had the distinction of recasting the most famous bell of all, Big Ben weighing 13½ tons and today the third heaviest in the kingdom. The exact weight of the original bell which had cracked in New Palace Yard the previous year may be ascertained from the entry in the foundry's ledger dated 28 May 1858 which gives the figure as 15 tons 13cwt 2qtr 19lb. A table comparing the weights of Britain's heaviest bells has been included in Appendix V.

The man responsible for recasting Big Ben was Thomas Kimber. He was about thirty years old at the time and was obviously very gifted for he also painted for Robert Stainbank, Mears' future partner, a watercolour depicting the Great Bell being admired by George Mears, his wife and daughter. This painting now hangs proudly in the company's office.

The twentieth century saw the foundry continue its fine work. In 1938/9 a magnificent ring of twelve bells was cast for Liverpool (Anglican) Cathedral. A thirteenth bell was also provided which allows for ringing to take place on just eight of the bells, but in a different key. With a tenor weighing 4 tons, heavier than even the largest of Big Ben's quarter bells, they form the heaviest ringing peal in the world. The foundry was especially busy just after the Second World War as bombing raids had caused the loss of several rings, and Whitechapel provided new bells for many of the London churches. These included Bow Bells at St Mary le Bow and the 'Oranges and Lemons' peal at St Clement Danes.

An article in *The Ringing World*, the weekly journal for church bell-ringers, recently drew attention to a book of nursery rhymes published in 1744 under the title *Tommy Thumb's Pretty Song Book*. This included an early form of the 'Oranges and Lemons' rhyme but billed as 'London Bells' and starting with the lines:

> Two Sticks and an Apple,
> Ring ye Bells at Whitechapple . . .

Note the original spelling and the wording – the modern version has '*say* the bells *of*'. Could it be that this little-known first verse refers to the foundry? It might; after all, the business had recently moved into the Whitechapel Road.

A ring of ten bells was cast for the National Cathedral in Washington in 1964 and in 1971 a ring of ten was cast for Westminster Abbey. The celebrated Bicentennial Bell weighing just over 5½ tons was cast as a gift from Britain to the people of the United States in 1976, since when it has resided in the Independence National Historic Park in Philadelphia. Although bellfounding remains a traditional craft, the twentieth century brought many changes, not only to the way in which bells are designed and fitted but also in their method of production, and this resulted in the complete rebuilding of the company's engineering workshops during the 1980s.

One of the most enterprising projects in recent times has been the manufacture of the new ring of twelve cast for Canterbury Cathedral in 1981. The entire project, which covers twenty-one bells in three towers, was the most extensive bell restoration work undertaken in Britain since the Second World War. Two other notable rings have been one of twelve bells cast in 1988 for St Martin in the Fields in London and a ring of sixteen cast in 1991 for St Martin in the Bull Ring in Birmingham. Most recently, the foundry cast a bell as a gift from London to New York after the attacks in 2001.

The foundry prides itself not only on traditional craftsmanship but also on customer loyalty, which is legendary. Many parishes have relationships going back over many centuries and particular mention must be made of Westminster Abbey whose connection with the foundry dates from 1583.

But it is not just church and clock bells that are cast at Whitechapel. Since the middle of the eighteenth century the foundry has also produced sets of handbells and in recent years the pastime of handbell ringing has increased greatly in popularity, not only in Britain but also in the United States and Japan. The foundry's business is concerned with the design, manufacture and installation of bells from handbells weighing just a few ounces to church tower bells weighing many tons. Today, with few new churches under construction, and some even preferring to use tape recordings of peals, the demand for new bells is limited and much of their work involves repairing and recasting damaged bells and their fittings.

While being rightly proud of its impressive ancestry, the Whitechapel Bell Foundry is very much a forward-looking company. It has promoted the use of bell frames made from steel, and later from reinforced concrete and more recently has introduced a method of electronic bell tuning as well as supplying computerised electronic chiming devices.

Tours of the foundry are available, by appointment, where visitors are taken behind the scenes and given the opportunity of having the founding process explained.

Appendix III

THE ASTRONOMER ROYAL'S SPECIFICATION

Conditions to be observed in regard to the construction of the clock of the New Palace of Westminster

I. Relating to the Workmanlike Construction of the Clock.

1. The clock-frame is to be of cast-iron, and of ample strength. Its parts are to be firmly bolted together. Where there are broad bearing surfaces, these surfaces are to be planed.
2. The wheels are to be of hard bell metal, with steel spindles working in bell-metal bearings, and proper holes for oiling the bearings. The teeth of the wheels are to be cut to form on the epicycloidal principle.
3. The wheels are to be so arranged that any one can be taken out without disturbing the others.
4. The pendulum pallets are to be jewelled.

II. Relating to the accurate going of the Clock

5. The escapement is to be dead-beat, or something equally accurate, the recoil escapement being expressly excluded.
6. The pendulum is to be compensated.
7. The train of wheels is to have a remontoir action, so constructed as not to interfere with the dead-beat principle of the escapement.

8. The clock is to have a going fusee.

9. It will be considered an advantage if the external minute hand has a discernible motion at certain definite seconds of time.

10. A spring apparatus is to be attached for accelerating the pendulum at pleasure during a few vibrations.

11. The striking machinery is to be so arranged that the first blow for each hour shall be accurate to a second of time.

III. Relating to the possible Galvanic Connexion with Greenwich

12. The striking detente is to have such parts that, whenever need shall arise, one of the two following plans may be adopted, (as, after consultation with Mr. Wheatstone* or other competent authorities, shall be judged best;) either that the warning movement may make contact, and the striking movement break contact, for a battery, or that the striking movement may produce a magneto-electric current.

13. Apparatus shall be provided which will enable the attendant to shift the connexion, by means of the clock action, successively to different wires of different hours, in case it should hereafter be thought desirable to convey the indications of the clock to several different places.

IV. General Reference to the Astronomer Royal

14. The plans, before commencing the work, and the work when completed, are to be subjected to the approval of the Astronomer Royal.

* Charles Wheatstone was a gifted scientist and inventor. In 1837 he patented a system for transmitting signals to distant places by means of electric currents.

15. In regard to the Articles 5 to 11, the maker is recommended to study the construction of the Royal Exchange Clock.

22 June 1846.   [signed] G.B. Airy

An extra condition was added in 1847:

16. The hour wheel is to carry a ratchet-shape wheel or a succession of cams, which will break contact with a powerful magnet, at least as often as once a minute for the purpose of producing a magneto-electric current, that will regulate other clocks in the New Palace.

Note: This is the specification that was drawn up by George Airy, the Astronomer Royal, in 1846. The original spelling has been retained.

Most clockmakers believed that the specification set impossible demands for such a large turret clock.

Appendix IV

DIMENSIONS OF THE GREAT CLOCK AND BELLS

The Clock Tower:

Height of finial	316ft
Height of centre of each dial	180ft
Height of belfry	205ft
Height of Ayrton Light	250ft
Width of clock tower	40ft
Steps to clock room	290
Steps to belfry	334

The Mechanism:

Designer	Edmund Beckett Denison
Maker	Started by Edward Dent, completed on his death by his stepson Frederick Dent
Built	1852–4
Installed in clock room	1859
Weight	5 tons
Length of bedplate	15ft 5in
Width of bedplate	4ft 11in
Escapement	Grimthorpe double three-legged
Length of pendulum (to centre of gravity)	13ft
Overall length of pendulum	14ft 6in
Weight of pendulum (including bob)	6cwt
Weight of pendulum bob	4cwt

Going train weight	5cwt
Striking train weight	1 ton
Chiming train weight	1 ton 5cwt

The Dials:

Number of dials	4
Diameter of each dial	23ft
Weight of each dial	4 tons
Number of glass panes in each dial	312
Length of each figure	2ft
Length of each minute hand	14ft
Length of each hour hand	9ft
Weight of each minute hand (with counterpoise)	2cwt
Weight of each hour hand (with counterpoise)	6cwt

The Bells:

Hour bell: note E (Big Ben)

Height	7ft 6in
Diameter	9ft
Weight	13 tons 10cwt 3qtr 15lb
Weight of striking hammer	4cwt

Quarter bells (the chimes):

First note G sharp

Diameter	3ft 9in
Weight	1 ton 1cwt

Second note F sharp

Diameter	4ft
Weight	1 ton 6cwt

Third note E

Diameter	4ft 6in
Weight	1 ton 13cwt

Fourth note B

Diameter	6ft
Weight	3 tons 18cwt

Appendix V

BRITAIN'S HEAVIEST BELLS

1. Great Paul
Bourdon bell of St Paul's Cathedral, London
John Taylor & Co., Loughborough, 1881
Weight 16 tons 14cwt 2qtr 19lb
Note E flat

2. Great George
Bourdon bell of Liverpool (Anglican) Cathedral
John Taylor & Co., Loughborough, 1938
Weight 14 tons 15cwt 2qtr 2lb
Note C sharp

3. Big Ben
Hour bell of the Great Clock of the Royal Palace of
    Westminster, London
Whitechapel Bell Foundry, London, 1858
Weight 13 tons 10cwt 3qtr 15lb
Note E
(Recast from original bell made at Stockton-on-Tees by John
    Warner & Sons, Cripplegate, London, 1856 Weight 15 tons
    13cwt 2qtr 19lb)

4. Great Peter
Bourdon bell of York Minster
John Taylor & Co., Loughborough, 1927

Weight 10 tons 16cwt 2qtr 22lb
Note E flat
(Recast from original bell made by Whitechapel Bell Foundry,
 London, 1845 Weight 10 tons 14lb)

5. **Little John**
Hour bell of the clock of Nottingham Council House
John Taylor & Co., Loughborough, 1927
Weight 10 tons 7cwt 27lb
Note E flat

Chronology

At the outset I had imagined that there would be an official record of the clock's history. This turned out not to be the case and the following has been drawn from various sources. It is probably not complete and a few dates are uncertain, nevertheless it does provide a good picture of the more important events before and during the life of the Great Clock.

late 1200s	First great clock erected at Westminster. Great Tom, the hour bell, cast weighing 4 tons
1580 6 April	Earthquake felt in south-eastern England during early evening. Clock escapes damage but Great Tom is set ringing by the tremor
1640s	Clock sustains damage during Civil War but remains in service
1656 25 December	Christiaan Huygens completes design for pendulum clock
1675	Royal Observatory established at Greenwich by Charles II
late 1600s	Clock lapses into deplorable state
1698	Clock pulled down, Great Tom sold to St Paul's Cathedral but falls from carriage en route and is shattered
1716	After two unsuccessful attempts, Great Tom recast by Whitechapel Bell Foundry. Weight increased to 4 tons 12cwt 14lb

1793	New clock erected at Great St Mary's University Church, Cambridge by Thwaites of London. Cambridge quarters introduced
1833	Time ball erected at Royal Observatory, Greenwich
1834	Fire destroys Palace of Westminster.
16 October	Parliament is prorogued and Select Committee formed to consider rebuilding and to issue invitations to architects to enter an open competition for design of new palace
1836 28 April	Charles Barry's design for new Houses of Parliament (including clock) accepted by Select Committee
1838 10 January	Fire destroys Royal Exchange
1840	E.J. Dent & Company founded
1843 28 September	Construction of clock tower begins
1844	Plans for elevation for new Palace of Westminster exhibited at the Royal Academy
1845	Clock erected by Edward Dent at the rebuilt Royal Exchange. Initially the chimes play an incorrect form of the Cambridge quarters
1846	George Airy, Astronomer Royal, asked to referee design of Great Clock
1846 22 June	Airy draws up specification for Great Clock. This requires that the first blow of each hour be struck within a second of the time
1848	Bill before Parliament to standardise time in the United Kingdom, but thrown out
1848 May	Edmund Beckett Denison, barrister and expert on horology, asked to act as joint referee for design of Great Clock
1852 January	Contract let to Edward Dent. Work begins on mechanism

1852 14 September	Augustus Welby Pugin dies
1853 8 March	Edward Dent dies. Turret clockmaking division of business passes to his stepson Frederick Dent
1854 January	Benjamin Louis Vulliamy dies
1854	Clock mechanism completed
1855 April	After several months of testing the mechanism in Dent's workshop, Airy announces his satisfaction with clock's performance
1855 July	Sir Benjamin Hall appointed Chief Commissioner of Works
1856 6 August	Big Ben I cast by John Warner & Sons of Cripplegate at their Stockton on Tees foundry. Bell found to weigh almost 16 tons
1856 21 October	Big Ben I arrives in London
1856 October	Four quarter bells cast by Warners at Cripplegate
1857 17 October	Big Ben I cracks after many months of testing in New Palace Yard
1858 February	Sir Benjamin Hall ceases to be Chief Commissioner of Works; succeeded by Lord John Manners
1858 17 February	Big Ben I broken up in New Palace Yard
1858 10 April	Big Ben recast by the Whitechapel Bell Foundry. Weight of bell reduced to 13 tons 10cwt 3qtr 15lb
1858 12 October	Big Ben II raised to the belfry
1859 31 May	Clock started officially, though silent and with hands on just two dials
1859 11 July	Hourly strike introduced
1859 7 September	Quarter chimes introduced

1859 1 October	Big Ben II cracks, clock silent again
1860	Frederick Dent dies
1860 12 May	Sir Charles Barry dies
1860	Temporary chime introduced. Hours struck on largest quarter bell
1862	Big Ben returned to service, Westminster chimes restored
1863	Electromagnetic link established to Royal Observatory, Greenwich for comparing clock's accuracy
1867 27 April	Sir Benjamin Hall dies
1880	Definition of Time Act establishes Greenwich Mean Time as legal standard throughout United Kingdom
1884	Prime Meridian Treaty ratified, reckoning longitude from Greenwich
1885	Ayrton Light, visible only in west London, installed
1892	Little Ben erected outside Victoria station
1892/3	Present Ayrton Light, with all round visibility, installed
1893	Present clock erected at St Paul's Cathedral by John Smith of Derby
1910 May	Big Ben tolled for death of King Edward VII
1916	Bells silenced for remainder of First World War
1916	Daylight Saving Act introduced; clocks advanced by one hour during summer months
1918 11 November	Bells returned to service at 11 a.m. to announce end of hostilities
1923 21 April	Frank Hope-Jones broadcasts first BBC radio 'time signal' from his own watch
1923 31 December	First radio broadcast welcomes the new year from microphone set up on roof of nearby building

1924 5 February	Greenwich Time Signal introduced
1924 17 February	First regular broadcast. Microphone installed in belfry
1931 September	Clock tower floodlit for Illumination Congress
1932 19 December	Empire Broadcasting Service inaugurated. Big Ben now heard overseas
1934	Clock out of service for major overhaul. Great Tom broadcasts time on the radio from 30 April until 3 July
1935 May	Clock tower floodlit for Silver Jubilee of King George V
1936 February	Big Ben tolled for death of King George V
1936 24 July	Post Office Speaking Clock (TIM) introduced
1936 23 September	Clock stopped by painter's ladder resting against one of the driveshafts
1939 1 September	Clock lights and Ayrton Light extinguished at outbreak of Second World War
1940	Link to Greenwich destroyed by enemy action. Clock's performance no longer compared with Observatory
1940 10 November	Remembrance Sunday. Big Ben Minute introduced on Home Service at 9 p.m.
1941 10/11 May	Clock tower hit during air raid. South dial completely shattered but clock's accuracy unaffected
1941 3 June	Carpenter's hammer left on mechanism stops clock
1944 16 June	Live transmission suspended. Gramophone recordings of the bells transmitted from Broadcasting House
1944 8 September	Live transmission resumed
1944 9 December	Suspension spring breaks, stopping clock

233

1945 25 January	Rubber bushes on quarter bell hammers freeze and muffle chimes. At 9 p.m. listeners hear one quarter bell then three or four 'thumps' from bell hammers followed by Greenwich Time Signal
1945 24 April	Ayrton Light relit
1945 30 April	Clock lights switched on at end of hostilities
1945 8 May	Clock tower floodlit for VE Day
1947 28/29 January	Rubber bushes on quarter bell hammers freeze and muffle chimes. At midnight listeners hear a few notes of chimes, one stroke, then silence
1949 12 August	Early evening. Starlings land on minute hand slowing clock by five minutes. Unable to broadcast at 9 p.m. but correct by midnight
1949 31 December	First television broadcast welcomes the new year from cameras mounted on roof of St Thomas' Hospital
1951	Clock tower floodlit for Festival of Britain and every summer since
1952 February	Big Ben tolled for death of King George VI
1955 13 January	Early morning. Clock stopped by build up of snow on ledges beneath dials
1955 18 July	Striker rope breaks. Clock does not strike from 10 a.m. until 5 p.m. but chimes as normal
1956	Major overhaul. Great Tom broadcasts time on the radio from 2 July until 23 December
1956 11 November	Remembrance Sunday. Clock still stopped under overhaul and absent from ceremony at 11 a.m.
1957 28 May	Clock stopped by paint pot left on girder catching counterweight of hour hand. Unable to broadcast at 9 p.m.

1959 3 June	11 a.m. Centenary commemoration in New Palace Yard
1959 June–September	Centenary exhibition staged in the Jewel Tower. Orb and shower floodlit
1960 17 September	9 p.m. Final Big Ben Minute, thereafter news moves to 10 p.m. and BBC fades strokes
1961 31 December	Noon. Clock slowed 10 minutes by snow on hands. Corrected well before midnight for striking in new year
1964	Little Ben taken down for repairs
1965 30 January	Clock silent for Churchill's funeral from 9.45 a.m. until midnight
1966 22 June	Clock chimes the quarters but does not strike the hours as winding motor overwinds striking train. Correct by 6 p.m. on 23 June
1968 9 January	Early morning. Clock stopped by build up of snow on ledges beneath dials
1970 3 April	Final broadcast at 10 p.m. on Radio 4 (formerly Home Service). Thereafter replaced by Greenwich Time Signal.
1971	Thwaites & Reed take over maintenance of clock from E.J. Dent
1972 1 January	Greenwich Time Signal revised. The final pip, which denotes the time, lengthened for identification
1976 5 August	3.45 a.m. Clock suffers major catastrophe as metal fatigue destroys part of the chiming mechanism and causes considerable damage to rest of movement. Clock is started the same day and resumes striking after a few weeks but chimes remain silent for nine months. Great Tom and Big Ben broadcast time on radio

1976 31 December	Chimes still silent, so clock can only strike in the new year
1977 4 May	Clock returned to full working order as Queen visits Palace of Westminster for Silver Jubilee Loyal Address
1977	Exhibition relating to disaster held in Westminster Hall
1981 15 December	Little Ben re-installed after major overhaul
1983 March	Scaffolding erected around clock tower in preparation for extensive cleaning programme which will last for two years. One face is covered and cleaned at a time, leaving the others visible with clock going and bells sounding as usual
1984 11 June	Greenpeace protesters climb scaffolded clock tower to demonstrate against nuclear testing
1985 5 June	Ceremony held at south clock face on completion of cleaning
1986 March	Rubber bush on largest quarter bell hammer freezes and muffles chime
1987 January	Rubber bushes on quarter bell hammers freeze and muffle chimes
1987 24/25 October	Cracks found in striking mechanism during routine maintenance at change back to GMT. Hour bell silent for one week
1990 5 February	BBC takes over Greenwich Time Signal
1990 March	Hour bell taken out of service as metal fatigue discovered in striking hammer arm. Clock continues to chime quarters
1990 29 August	New hammer arm fitted, clock resumes striking. BBC claims new hammer arm has altered tone and refuses to broadcast bell

1990 22 December	Broadcasting resumed
1994	Engineers pump hundreds of tons of concrete under clock tower to protect from tunnelling for Jubilee Line
1997 30 April	Clock stops for 45 minutes due to fault with escapement bearing. Omen for General Election next day?
1999	Multicoloured light show on the dials and switching on and off in time with the bells is planned for New Year's Eve for the so-called start of the new millennium, with commercial logos projected on to clock face. Idea of logos rejected immediately and light show abandoned
2002 March	Parliamentary Works Directorate takes over maintenance from Thwaites & Reed
2002 11 November	Remembrance Day (Monday). Visitors to the belfry heard over the air as clock broadcasts 11 a.m. strike
2004 20 March	Two Greenpeace protesters scale clock tower in demonstration over Iraq war
2004 29 April	12.45 a.m. Locking lever on chiming mechanism fractures due to metal fatigue. Chimes silent for ten days but clock continues going and striking. Clock replaced over the air by Greenwich Time Signal
2004 9 May	New locking lever fitted, clock resumes chiming

Notes and References

CHAPTER 1

page 3   Earthquake in 1580: Very few British earthquakes
           have ever resulted in death. Roger Musson,
           'Fatalities in British Earthquakes', *Astronomy and
           Geophysics* (Journal of the Royal Astronomical
           Society), Vol. 44 (1) (February 2003), p. 14.

page 4   Sentry claims to hear Great Tom from Windsor:
           This story may be no more than apocryphal.
           (Anon.), 'Great Tom takes over from Big Ben',
           Radio Times, 1–7 July 1956, p. 3.

page 6   History of Greenwich Observatory: Colin A. Ronan
           (ed.), *Greenwich Observatory – 300 Years of
           Astronomy*, Times Books, 1975.

page 8   Development of Harrison's chronometers: Dava
           Sobel, *Longitude*, Fourth Estate, 1996.

page 14   The One o'Clock Gun: Iain Mackenzie, 'The One
           o'Clock Gun', *Horological Journal* (Journal of the
           British Horological Institute), December 1980, p. 24
           and Tom McKay, *What Time Does Edinburgh's One
           o'Clock Gun Fire?*, available from Edinburgh Castle.

CHAPTER 2

page 25   *the striking machinery is to be so arranged . . .*
Astronomer Royal's Specification. George Airy,
'Conditions to be observed in regard to the
construction of the clock of the New Palace of
Westminster', 1846. (The specification is
reproduced in full in Appendix III, p. 221.)

page 27   *It is impossible for me to consider Mr Vulliamy . . .*
Letter from George Airy, Astronomer Royal to Lord
Morpeth, Chief Commissioner of Works, May 1847.

page 39   Inscription on the original bell: John Darwin, *The
Triumphs of Big Ben*, Robert Hale, 1986, p. 15.

CHAPTER 4

page 69   *So ends the history of the clock up to the present
time . . .* Alfred Gillgrass, *The Book of Big Ben*,
Herbert Joseph, 1946, pp. 7–8.

CHAPTER 5

page 73   History of the Houses of Parliament: Bryan H. Fell
and K.R. Mackenzie, *The Houses of Parliament (A
Guide to the Palace of Westminster)*, HMSO, 1977.

page 78   Big Ben probably named after Sir Benjamin Hall:
Letter from Miss Maxwell Frazer in *The Times*,
3 March 1971, p. 13.

page 79   History of Great St Mary's University Church
(Anon.), *Great St Mary's, The University Church
Cambridge*, available from the church and C.M.
Ockelton, *Tower and Bells: The Tower, Bells &
Ringers of Great S. Mary's Church, Cambridge*,

The Society of Cambridge Youths, 1981; available through the church.

page 84   Public clocks and their chimes (Anon.), 'The Song of the Hours', *Horological Journal*, December 1941, p. 378.

CHAPTER 6

page 93   *I have tried your escapement in the most malicious way* . . . John Darwin, *The Triumphs of Big Ben*, Robert Hale, 1986, p. 109.

page 95   *as it is not patented* . . . T.R. Robinson, 'How Grimthorpe's Gravity Escapement was designed', *Horological Journal*, June 1959, p. 352.

CHAPTER 7

page 109   Frank Hope-Jones commenting on the Greenwich Time Signal: Donald de Carle, *Teach Yourself Horology*, English Universities Press, 1965, p. 73.

CHAPTER 8

page 125   Wartime damage to Houses of Parliament: Bryan H. Fell and K.R. Mackenzie, *The Houses of Parliament (A Guide to the Palace of Westminster)*, HMSO, 1977.

CHAPTER 9

page 140   Substitution of Great Tom for Big Ben: 'Great Tom takes over from Big Ben', *Radio Times*, 1–7 July 1956, p. 3.

CHAPTER 10

page 160 Preview of Big Ben's 100th birthday (Anon.), *Radio Times*, 31 May–6 June 1959, p. 4.

CHAPTER 13

page 201 The length of the second: *Explanatory Supplement to the Astronomical Almanac*, University Science Books, 1992, p. 40.

page 205 Compact disc (sound recording of twelve and one o'clock strikes plus quarter chimes). *Sound Effects of England*, BBC, CD867, 1994.

Website providing sound of bells every fifteen minutes. www.ukonline.co.uk

APPENDIX II

page 218 *Two Sticks and an Apple* (nursery rhyme possibly referring to Whitechapel Bell Foundry). (Anon.), 'Oranges and Lemons Book Makes £40,000', *Ringing World* (Journal for Church Bell-Ringers), 25 January 2002, p. 73.

Bibliography

BOOKS AND GUIDES

Big Ben and the Clock Tower, London, Her Majesty's Stationery Office, 1987 (revised 2002)

Big Ben and the Westminster Clock Tower, London, Pitkin, 1997

Big Ben: Its Engineering Past and Future, London, Engineering Sciences Division of the Institution of Mechanical Engineers, 1981

Darwin, John, *The Triumphs of Big Ben*, London, Robert Hale, 1986

Denison, Edmund Beckett, *A Rudimentary Treatise on Clocks, Watches and Bells*, London; reprinted E.P. Publishing, 1974

Fell, Bryan H. and Mackenzie, K.R., *The Houses of Parliament (A Guide to the Palace of Westminster)*, London, Her Majesty's Stationery Office, 1977

Gillgrass, Alfred, *The Book of Big Ben*, London, Herbert Joseph, 1946

Great St Mary's, The University Church Cambridge (available from the church)

McKay, Tom, *What Time Does Edinburgh's One o'Clock Gun Fire?* (available from Edinburgh Castle)

Ockelton, C.M., *Tower and Bells: The Tower, Bells & Ringers of Great S. Mary's Church, Cambridge*, Society of Cambridge Youths, 1981 (available from the church)

Phillips, Alan, *The Story of Big Ben*, London, Her Majesty's Stationery Office, 1959

Ronan, Colin A. (ed.), *Greenwich Observatory – 300 Years of Astronomy*, London, Times Books, 1975

Saunders, Ann, *The Royal Exchange*, Guardian Royal Exchange, 1991

Sobel, Dava, *Longitude*, London, Fourth Estate, 1996

PAPERS AND ARTICLES

Bateman, D.A. and James, K., 'The Pendulum of Big Ben', *Horological Journal*, February 1977

Crampton, F.J.P., '"Big Ben" – the Final Chapter', *Horological Journal*, September 1981

Darwin, J.F.B., 'The day time stood still', *Horological Journal*, May–July 1988 (in three parts)

'Little Ben has returned to Victoria', *Horological Journal*, January 1982

Mackenzie, Iain, 'The "One o'Clock Gun"', *Horological Journal*, December 1980

'Oranges and Lemons book makes £40,000', *Ringing World*, 25 January 2002

Robinson, T.R., '"Big Ben" and "Great Tom" – and their clocks', *Horological Journal*, February and March 1957 (in two parts)

—— 'The Great Westminster Clock Ticks Off a Century', *Horological Journal*, May–July 1959 (in three parts)

'The Song of the Hours', *Horological Journal*, December 1941

Wilding, J. 'The Westminster Tower Clock', *Horological Journal*, October 1976

—— 'The Westminster Tower Clock', *Horological Journal*, June 1977

Index